PRITENI

(B/PRITENI)

The Decimation of the Indigenous Keltic Britons

PRITENI |

THE DECIMATION OF THE INDIGENOUS CELTIC BRITONS

© Ly de Angeles. All rights reserved. No part of this book may be used, reproduced, stored in a retrieval system or transmitted in any form or by any means, electronic, mechanical, photocopying, scanning, recording, including Internet usage, without written permission from the author except in the case of brief quotations embodied in critical articles and reviews.

INGRAM SPARK AUSTRALIA
ISBN – 9780648502531

Cover – The Albion/LeStrange Family

To contact the author – www.lydeangeles.com

PRELUDE

Somewhere, somehow, and by someone, a beginning must be made ~~ Séamas Fionntán Ó Leathlobhair Revolutionary, 1807 – 1849 Ireland

PRITENI (P/Britenneh) is written in the present tense, and the first person, with the intent it be inclusive of us, as a people, indigenous to pre-Roman Britain (the p/briteneh, painted people) still alive in the twenty first century of the current era. Of our language, culture, clothing, music, ancestral lineage, little is known. Our mysticism (extant) and spirituality are explored to the depths I am able, in the understanding that the knowledge of such provides psychic sovereignty and cultural insight. The dates here are approximate as they are estimated by the Julian calendar.

Note – the author's ancestor is CARADOC, and itis the *only* name of the Keltic people not reproduced in phonetic language, except once for context.

PRE-BEGINNING

Before we write of the priteni people, and the destruction of our culture, we take you into the monumental depths of time, for perspective. we would have you dwell, for a moment, on Stonehenge, believed to have been built around five and a half thousand years ago. The Ridgeway, a trade route, between the Dorset coast and the land of the Ekeneh People on the farthest east coast near modern day Norfolk. This road has been in use for at least five thousand years.

Avebury. That stone circle is one of the largest in all of Europe. It has an outer ring of upright stones and two inner rings. Its landscape, contains the West Kennett Long Barrow and one of the Severn-Cotswold *tombs* (potentially not tombs at all but closed initiatory spaces), was built at least four and a half thousand years ago. Silbury Hill, the tallest human-made monument of its kind in Europe is constructed of chalk, its purpose long-forgotten.

The Callanish Stones on the Isle of Lewis, in the Outer Hebrides (where golden eagles, seals and red deer still run free), with its secret central burial chamber and surrounding ritual avenue. It is one of the oldest teasers of all, standing there, at the edge of the world, for easily five thousand years. Why? The Rollright Stones, three monuments built at different times, between two and four thousand years ago. Swinside, Whitehawk Camp. The White Horse of Uffington carved into the earth and filled with chalk anywhere between 100CE and a thousand years before this current era, in the Bronze Age, most clearly visible by air. Who did this? What does it mean? Why?

Long Meg and her Daughters, another close initiatory chamber, the Serpent Stone at Aberlemno in Alba (Scotland) with its carved sigils, inscrutable except to guesswork, Newgrange, in Ireland, erected around six thousand years ago, and accurately aligned to the first sun of midwinter, as also is Stonehenge. The same labyrinth design, carved onto the cliffs of Cornwall

(Kernow), that lies beneath the cathedral of Chartres. Thousands and thousands of hill forts, barrows and dolmens (we've been here a very long time). More have recently been discovered at Durrington Walls[1] near Stonehenge. The hunt for crop circles that recently led aerial mappers to discover massive numbers of humanly constructed barrow mounds, ceremonial walkways, camp settlements and circular holes in patterns that suggest wood henges, just as exist near Newgrange.

I speculate that these massive constructions and fortifications result from our ancestors' spiritual connectedness to Earth. That perhaps crop circles[2] have been with us since the Neolithic period when it is theorized that the first menhirs[3] were raised.

That, as Dr. Lynne Kelly suggests, in her definitive

---

[1] http://www.dailymail.co.uk/sciencetech/article-1296749/Stonehenge-twin-Archaeologists-discover-wooden-henge-site.html
[2] There is a reference to crop circles as early as 1686 in Robert Plott's book *A Natural History of Staffordshire* in which he alludes to "fairy rings", seeking sources 28 June 2015.
[3] Standing stone

book *The Memory Code*. The vast hand-dug chalk ditches, surrounding so many of these seemingly impossible constructions, are more than mere thirty foot deep and wide flat-bottomed water catchment areas, considering they are porous and dug by hand, intentionally, with antler -bone.

Dr. Kelly suggests they were open gathering grounds for oratory, story-telling and song. Anyone serious about this research into antiquity I seriously suggest her book.

Stone circles and monuments are everywhere. Not burial mounds but chambers of initiation and the telling of undiluted lore. Once we listened.

MAP OF THE INDIGENOUS TERRITORIES

For original, full size document copy/paste: https://commons.wikimedia.org/wiki/File%3A1865_Spruner_Map_of_the_British_Isles_(England%2C_Scotland%2C_Ireland)_-_Geographicus_-_Britannia-spruner-1865.jpg

PART 1

CHAPTER ONE

In a country occupied by immigrants, slaves and their descendants, we are all displaced people, searching for roots and a sense of belonging...

Walking the Maze, Loren Cruden.

55BCE – THE FIRST INVASION (JULIUS CAESAR)

At the time of the first invasion by Rome, under the emperor Julius Caesar, it is late summer, the season of plenty. Rome deploys a reconnaissance-in-force. An invasion that fails, it is, however, Rome's foot in the door. Our seers warned us they were coming.

From across the Narrow Sea, they said. They'll try to land their ships along the coast of the Belgae. White cliffs and in accessible coves.

And there they are. Through the fading late morning fog and watery, silver sun. Eighty ships unable to make landfall.

We are twelve thousand warriors. Men, women and initiated youth who have had their first kill, bonded to hound, horse or hawk, trained in battle. We line the headland and cliff tops daring them to come ashore. Chieftains of five great nations hold twelve foot high spears, bearing the skulls of our ancestors painted red with the ochre of life. Pennants of horsehair, chests and breasts blue with tattoos, slick with bear fat colored silver with ash[4]. Breeches of otter, seal or marmot and decorated with bronze and iron. Boots of soft leather through which to feel the bellies of the horses, sensitive to every psychic thought.

Who are we? Kashivellanesh, lean and fair, his beard and moustaches red as the glow of fire, hair dark with clay, piled high onto his head and held up with gold twigs. Tanned bear skin over his shoulders,

---
[4] Isatis tinctoria

a ready smile at any woman horsed nearby, torques aplenty and jet threaded with gold through his earlobes. He is wosaljaxto[5] of the Kashuvalluneh people. With him, in chariots or astride the four pillared saddles, is Kloutābona, *wosaljaxto* of the Dur-ratrijeh, small woman, but fierce and dark, her mother of the Silures tribe in the mountains to the west. Kloutābona is flanked by two of her husbands, and several massive hounds gifted to her by the Kalledonneh at the time of the wedding to her principal husband, one of the highest-ranking chieftains of that clan. The Trinovanteh are represented, the Kanteh where the ships are likely to sail next and the Ekeneh, of course, neighbor of the Kashuvalluneh.

Out to sea Roman orders are shouted in an alien tongue. Hand gestures speak between craft, their meanings inscrutable. A hundred pair of oars, on each of the smaller vessels, cut through the deep water turning their boats. The sails change tack on the

---

[5] *Chieftain*. Proto Keltic.

larger.

They sail north, and we follow. All day and into the afternoon.

Until, at the pink and silver of sundown, the fleet bunch, drop anchor and lower their sails, floating like a huddle of ducks in the deep water, a hundred yards from the sands that leads to the stronghold of the Kanteh.

We have sent for reinforcements, requests to the furthest fortresses, and they arrive before full dark. We descend to the beachhead and surrounding forest.

Kashivellanesh, Kloutābona and several other chieftains, drive their chariots onto the sand, whooping and ululating, to join the war bands by the ocean edge.

Kashivellanesh' father, Helyesh, whilst having bequeathed the title of chieftain onto his son, remains a fierce and revered elder. He leads several hundred people from the north. He is still powerful and a terrifying sight. His iron grey hair drips with bear grease and is heavy-laden with kill feathers and talismans, and tipped with the many bronze hoops signifying druid training. With him are warriors, their cooks, their hunters and their seers. They swell our numbers substantially. We join the Shejoveh, and the other three chieftains of our brothers and sisters of the Kanteh, whose lands Caesar seeks to access.

The Romans are bothered. They cannot come closer because the tide is receding rapidly, and they know it. Should they tempt fate they will strand. But should they do so we will make them ghosts in a strange country, doomed to wander, lost and confused, amongst our own.

Legionaries and auxiliaries darken the railings while men in gold helmets, with red or black bristles aligned tidily along the top (like our hair, really. No wait, ours is much better), scarlet cloaks and molded breastplates, short swords in curiously interesting scabbards, embossed shields hanging from slack hands. We can see their eyes from here. They are smiling, or looking down noses, like beaks.

We thunder our horses and chariots up and down along the shingles, yelling, *Come on! You want us? Come on! And, Go on, go back! Fuck off to where you came from*!

A blast from a horn and their men appear poised to leap from the ships despite—or perhaps because of—the ocean ebb. We rain the first of our spears. They take their toll. Do not come here, we demand. Turn and leave our lands. But they do not. They return fire.

Someone carrying a golden standard topped by a gilded eagle jumps into Manannán mac Lír[6] like an idiot, blowing a little trumpet, summoning his brothers in arms to follow. We are stunned. I don't believe it. They are crazy. Infantry take to the shallow

---

[6] Ocean

water in two waves of thousands, their lightweight armor on their upper bodies, funny metal hats, little skirts over brown legs, bare other than boots, carrying standards, shields and short swords, soundless within the roar of our battle cries. They die and colour the ocean scarlet.

Some make it, safe under the sheets of arrows that try to hold us at bay.

Druids raise song, their shadow women calling with the voices of ravens, answered from the forests by a thousand feathered sentinels, *Send us this banquet*, they joke. Seers from the *tuaths* invoke spirits of the wild water because it is rude to enter when we are uninvited. We smell its welcome, as Manannán mac Lír makes the sand suck at the strangers' boots, keeping them slow and unwieldy.

Two, five, ten million blue soldier crabs dart from their little holes, in a frenzy of gorging, picking at the flesh in tiny nips and nibbles, and sucking in the blood already pooling in eddies and runnels. Then we attack.

We cut them down, but that first wave of military keep coming anyway, relentlessly. Caesar and those fellows in the fancy helmets, stay safely aboard ship, watching the slaughter with blank faces. The sea is black with blood and gore, bodies detritus upon the tide line. We back up the sand to the beach head. Perhaps now they will flee.

Commands are shouted. Code. The next wave reaches land, this time differently. They mass together, shields raised, short swords poking from between. They come at us. And come at us, and come. And come. Slaughter. That's okay. We are okay to die today.

But then fire falls from the sky. What is that? Kloutābona dies where she rides, struck from her horse by the full force of that projectile. She continues to burn until she is a blackness on the sand.

Ballista[7]. Their soldiers line the water's edge in a defensive formation of shields that we can' penetrate.

A curse on you. We will feast tonight, sharpen our swords, chronicle the events to the druids and sleep. That's enough for one day. We ride and run to the inland tuath of the Kanteh, leaving our dead to the gulls and ravens and tidal depths.

---

[7] weapon launcher.

CHAPTER TWO

Proud People Made to Fear

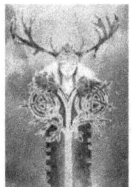

After the long twilight the mists finally move in from the sea and we send three hundred to see if the aliens have fled. They return with news that no, they have not gone. They are camped along the beach away from the scene of battle. What's worse is that not all our warriors we thought dead, are dead. There are cages, as though for bears, set up upon the deck of the largest of their ships. Our wounded are shackled both inside these cages, and chained to the outside. Prisoners of war. History will call them hostages.

Their camp is patrolled by sentries, day and night. Why are they still here? We will not stop until they return our own.

At night we hear screams. Our people don't scream. We are fearless. What do they do to cause that much terror?

We continue to harass them day and night. We will not stop until they are gone. Some of the prisoners they discard, for us to find.

Flayed alive, our women are raped and cut to pieces. Some, both men and women have their urethras sewn shut and are force fed wine until they die inside. Some burned.

For two thousand years we have been travelers and traders, as far as the underground cities of the Nabataea's in the desert, to the vivid colors of the people and sunsets of India, to those in the snows at the Roof of the World, and our cousins across the sea to the south that once thrashed Rome. We know what they have become, trying to be Hellenic. To be Sparta but lavishly. We know about their greed. We also know they are everywhere. Several of us speak a little of their language. They would suffer it to become the new trade tongue, currently ours. Is that why they are here? To humiliate us? We have traded with them for centuries. Why come? We've heard them denigrate our landscape as dreary, our people as barbarians.

After many weeks they send us Komyush, once a proud man of the fortress of Nehmet-uneh[8], the capital of the Atrebatesh just across the narrow sea in northern Gaul. He has been a servant of Rome since it subjugated his people. He comes dressed in their robes, bearing gifts of wine and jewelry, glass from which to drink mead, fine cloth.

We do not want your things, the Trinovanteh say. But unfortunately, the Kashuvalluneh say *hmm. What will we trade?*

---

[8] Pronounced neymet-oona, common nemeton

They will keep on coming, Komyush says. They will not ever stop. They will take your lands, your lives. Everything. You cannot stand against them.

Say you, we respond. Traitor.

No, he says, I had no choice.

What is there to understand? We will fight them, we will defeat them. We are millions.

You are warriors, he says, sadly.

What?

You are warriors.

Yes, of course. We are strong. and we are brave, and we are not afraid to fight and die.

They have soldiers, he continues. You matter to your clans and to each other. They are trained to not feel. They do not feel. They take orders. That is all. They obey. If they do not obey they lose everything.

That does not make sense, we say.

They have forgotten to be warriors, he explains. It has been bred out of them. Soldiers do nothing else.

Why are you here? we ask.

To deliver an ultimatum that you secede to Rome (become Roman basically, and benefit because of it) or not and suffer the consequences which, we are assured, will be annihilation.

We need Komyush, because he speaks their language better than anyone here. What can we do but parley with them? Meanwhile our druids and wizards plot with the weather, with the sea, to take this from our hands.

With a thousand warriors at our backs we ride with Kashivellanesh to Caesar.

You are to go, we demand.

No, he answers, sniffing with disdain. Thousands more troops—cavalry, infantry—are already on the way here. There will be no peace.

And he turns his back on us.

Four days later their troop and horse-carrying ships are in dire danger as the druid magic takes effect.

Savage storms lash the sea and the coastline. Gales raise the oceans up and threaten to swallow the enemy whole. Julius Caesar's ships are shattered along our coast. But, the spells have had a backlash, because now the Romans cannot leave.

Yet still they have our people prisoner, so we dare not destroy them for fear of the terror they will inflict before we do so. So, we wait. We watch as they repair what ships they can. Are they leaving? Is that it? Our magic. The weather. Every day becomes colder and more furious. They will starve.

They complete repair and are gone at midwinter.

We have spies back from across the narrow sea. Ah, now we know why they came. Caesar has been told to step down. His senate does not like him anymore. He is a dictator and a narcissist. His own people will murder him in nine years.

How is that first attack remembered? We must sing

the praises of the Katuvallunneh *wosaljaxto*, Kashivellanesh because he led us to sagely hold it all. All our lands, and all done in the correct fashion, in the way of the ancestors. Of us and every species.
With glory and savagery and art. During and since Caesar.

Time passes. Years. Kashivellanesh now wars against the Trinovanteh because, we have only recently discovered, they have become a 'client *reginrum*[9] to Rome, their chieftain Imanuentiwesh a Romanized *regi*[10]. Now he is an enemy to the priteni people. That's really very sad and annoying. I'm sure the forests will enjoy their juices, the same as any others, as they decompose. They have been trading for what they consider luxuries from the Roman way of life, glass and wine. Selling off their grain and slaves and hunting hounds.

---

[9] Roman/Saxon: kingdom

[10] Latin for the later Anglo-Saxon: king (*cyng*)

In pitched battle Kashivellanesh cuts Imanwentiwesh down and takes his head for our tuath. Because of this, and in fear of his soft little life, Mandubrakesh' son, Imanwentiwesh, runs into hiding. Self-imposed exile. To the embarrassment of the Trinovanteh.

What does he do? Worse still. He joins Caesar in Gaul.

CHAPTER THREE
Art

P/BRITENEH PEOPLE – WHO WE ARE

Caesar keeps a record. The *Bellum Gallicum*[11] In it he writes of this tribe to the east: *Ex his omnibus longe sunt humanissimi qui Cantium incolunt, quae regio est maritima omnis, neque multum a Gallica differunt consuetudine.* "...who differ but little from the Gauls..."

What does this mean? We are Kelts, the Gaul are Kelts. They wear gold and bronze, we wear gold and bronze. They produce fine pottery, as do we. Like us they have druid lore and law. Like us they pay homage to the connectedness of life: genius loci, the

---

[11] Gallic Wars, Books 1 – 8

essences: of blacksmithing, learning, healing, raiding, memorizing. Homage to the spirit of the hunt, to the voices of the ancient dead whose skulls, painted with ochre of every color, adorn the walls of our *tuaths*. Druids, healers, judges, witches, wisdom holders. Us. Kelts. The difference, later, is that they will be beaten. Submissive. They will be colonized. Eventually they will have no choice. Rome will lose them of themselves.

CRAFT

Gold, bronze, woad, jet, pearls, pelts of bear and wolf and stag and every beast we eat, weaponry and chariots. Our cattle are prized throughout the known world, our greatest wealth. The wound strands of gold, silver, bronze and copper that are the torques we wear at throat and arm are a measure of status but can also prevent the strike of an enemy's blade. Rings, ear jewelry, necklaces adorn men and women, *rí tuaithe* and slave. Our bronzes upon our saddles, the bosses of our shields, carved boar tusk and stag antler heirloom talismans, the gifts from a thousand year ago and a thousand travelled lands beyond this green island. Magnificent, jewel-encrusted hair pins and ornaments galore, gold and gemstones. Because we're vain and proud. It is appropriate. We dress our hair, as I have mentioned a little, in lime or clay. Style it to mimic the tails of horses or the bristles of boar. And it is never cut.

Brother and sister hound, rough-haired and tall, smile with pride as their children are born beside our own. They are hunters, trained with son and daughter when both are puppies, and can bring down the largest bull stag. Horses, shaggy, thick, strong and dark. Their bravery, within an uncertain and shifting landscape of fen, bog, fog, mountain range and the currents they must ford to take the mystics to Inish Môn, the druid isle, is to become, in the future, legendary.

The hunter, and golden eagle with which they hunt, born and housed together, the same with peregrine and falcon. Symbiotic. Greaves of badger hide, studded and banded with iron and gold, hung with carved wooden talismans.

We are people of the horse. The people of the iron blade. When we fight our enemies, as often happens, we ride naked into battle, our hair limed and white, standing tall and hung with talismans and kill feathers banded by many colors, our bodies greased warm with bear fat, shimmering, invisible when mixed with ash, shadows of night. Men and women side by side, our war cry terrible to our enemies' ears, the spirits of our lands writhing and whooping amongst us, our ancestors, always with us.

CUSTOMS

Our festivals are times when many tribes come together: when the salmon run, when the stag rut. At harvest when the nuts and berries and apples quicken, and we work like mad people to store it in time for the big freeze. It's also when we slaughter what cattle we can and run our pigs, on leashes crafted of rawhide, through the forests of ancient oak in search of truffles, edible fungus, and the mushrooms whose spirits inform our seers and druids. Kill the brother bull and boar and the sister badger. Strip them, tan the hides, shape, sharpen and carve the bones, dry the meat, bury it deep.

At the end of winter, the broom is cleared for the cattle and ten foot high pyres are built and lit. The now-stale winter bedding goes up in flames, the cattle enchanted betwixt huge blazes, the young branded with the symbols of clan, free to roam because here, in the territory of the Katuvallunneh, only a rare idiot would raid what's ours. At the height of summer, we marry, mate, feast and get pissed on anything fermented. When the apple blossom rains down, the calves come, and the geese return to the waterways. Every season a reason to celebrate. Or mourn. Music? The *karnyx*, pipes, flutes of bone, bronze hand bells, shields and hides as drums. The Shiluresh gave us the *crwth*[12]. Always there is singing. Haunted, evocative, summoning, songs of heroism, of enchantment, of legends and lore, or just because we are pissed.

---

[12] Form of lyre

In the future our instruments will be remembered but not played. Our lore not sung. Can't. We will lose our language.

In two thousand years all will seem so twee, so past, so archaic. We will be portrayed as yokels with no style. Dear mother bear, we gave the Romans soap. But for now, I can breathe and make love in the company of my kindred, on bearskins, with wolves and foxes and owls watching from the forest, beneath the same skies as will always be.

Two thousand years from now, however, not everyone is fooled. Writer Tom Cowan[13] will compare us to another tribal culture across the Atlantic and, many generations from now, their lands, also, are invaded, the people driven towards extinction, their languages, traditions, spirituality and cultures almost disappearing from existence.

---

[13] Fire in the Head, Shamanism and the Keltic Spirit, HarperCollins, USA, 1993

There are striking parallels between Celtic tribal life and that of Native Americans... As peoples who practice an indigenous, earth-centered spirituality, the Celts and Native Americans share many animistic practices, along with a common attitude and respect for the land and the spirits of the land.

That's us. And the magic. Initiators, seers, sorcerers, dreamers and druids. Laws complex and profound. The knowledge holders[14] recall of ancestral lineages, vast. Our poetry and memories vast. Who marries who? What tribes does this unite? How many husbands? How many wives? Our status, our offspring, our fosterage?

"Who differ but little from the Gauls..." A mere three years from now the chieftain of the Arverneh in Gaul, Verkinjetorax, a proud and colorful *wosaljaxteh*, renowned far and wide across all the Keltic lands,

---

[14] Brehon (judges and law-makers) and bards (singers, storytellers, rememberers). Both are druids

Will unite a sea of warriors in a bid to drive Rome into Manannán mac Lír, they pollute our holy wells, so.

They are defeated. But not all. In secret *tuaths* the mothers nail many, many Roman heads to their wall posts, dedicating them to the children yet to be. We know this because words and deeds of such greatness spread like wildfire. Yes, we boast. We are proud. Why not? Those warriors are truly epic. They will be remembered for thousands of years.

But the priteni tribes to the east of here, along the coast, the Kenteh... Not sure of the consequences of their relationship with Rome. They are different to us. Their food is different. They are a people of the grain.

To a degree so are the Ekeneh [15] but they are not yet, and only until the death of Brashetahesh [16] after the second invasion. The real invasion.

---

[15] Approximately Norfolk
[16] Budekeh's known husband, called Prasutagus.

THE SPIRIT WORLD

Is the world. Everything. Life. The crows that eat the bodies and the ants that feed the bears and spiders. The wolf and bear that eat the deer that's grazed on the grass where your great-grandmother' body fed every small creature and tree root that grew the berries that fed the goose that takes the memory of her a thousand miles away and leaves her seed upon a distant shore.

Oh, it's endless!

Thousands of years from now, preeminent scholar, Dr Anne Ross will write of us, "The Kelts were so completely engrossed with, and preoccupied by, their religion and its expression, that it was constantly and positively at the forefront of their lives."

THE DESCENDENT

Within a generation, however, I will marry into the Katuvallunneh peole and my grandfather will become Karedok[17], son of Kymbelineh [18] (Caradoc ap Cunobelinus) and you and I are still them after two thousand years. We have not changed. We are descended from other tribes in other lands, but they are of no consequence here.

LOCATION

Brijanteh lands are overshadowed by a vast and fecund mountain range we call Brijeh[19]. She is Earth. She feeds us, clothes us, provides us with stag, boar, bear, pigeon, salmon, eggs, honey for both cooking and mead, trees for building, fires and knowledge. One day, country that will be known as the Pennines.

---

[17] Called Caractacus by the Romans, Geoffrey of Monmouth based his Arthur on this man.
[18] His name means dog-strong *cuno* – hound, and *belenos* (sun/strong)
[19] The modern day Pennines

We drink from this mother's pure and pristine water. River and lake. We hunt in her valleys of mist. Gather hazelnuts. Ferment elderberries. Understand the language of oak and ash and thorn. Strip willow to ease ague. She provides every healing herb, medicine and poison we will ever need.

Thousand-year-old yew trees inform us of ancestors even the druids don't remember.

Otters. Raven lore. Owl lore. Oysters. Honeycomb. Springs and streams within the valleys, amongst the thyme and mountain sage. Soot from the bone fires, from the cauldron, for tattoos. Mixed with bear fat to make for silver, night-stealth cattle raids and duck trapping. Ash tree and yew for bow and arrow. We use these only for the hunt, though. It won't occur to us for a very long time to make them more powerful. For war.

To the southeast, the farthest shores, and north, in the borderlands of the Brijanteh, the people grow oats and barley, imported during the time of bronze from Anatolia[20], Egypt, Massillia[21] and Crete.

We are allied to the Catuvellauni. They are the largest of all the tribes other than my own, the Brijanteh. They are rich. These they trade with Rome and many other countries. From Rome, they import wine and olive oil, fine Italian pottery, silver and bronze drinking cups, enamel jewellery. And they mint vast numbers of gold coins in their capital, Kamulodden.

Unlike the Trinovanteh, however, they retain their sovereignty.

---

[20] Turkey
[21] Modern day Marseille, part of the Old Silk Road trade route

CHAPTER FOUR

Do Not Go Gentle Into That Good Night, Rage, Rage...
Excerpt, Dylan Thomas

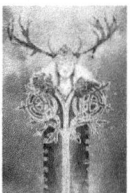

THE SECOND INVASION (JULIUS CAESAR)

The following year, Caesar embarks on a second incursion into the priteni people's lands and his military temporarily overpower the Catuvellauni, forcing them into retreat.

Unfortunately, this time, Mandubrakesh goes with them.

The Trinovanteh are, by now, embraced by Rome's wealth and privilege. They suck up to Caesar, bringing them into the bosom of Rome's praise. It seems that bullets and beads and sunken baths, roads of stone, the colour purple, mosaic, greater ease of international travel and extreme wealth, is quite an incentive for some. So, Caesar dubs Mandubrakesh *regi* of the Trinovanteh And Mandubrakesh forges treaties with Rome.

Does he really not comprehend the price? Invisibility? Disconnection from the ancestors and the spirit of the land? What we do know is the pieces on the board have strategically moved in favor of alien occupation.

Then Caesar departs again.

KATUVALLUNNEH

The Katuvallunneh are not beaten, however, and over the coming hundred years become more and more powerful until Kymbelineh ap Taskyavanesh becomes *wosaljaxto* at age eighteen. It is the year later known as 9CE. His black hair hangs loose to his hips, greased into ropes, his kill feathers from the snow goose that comes to the southern shores once a year, renowned for its endurance, gold and bronze ornaments dangling from the ends of the hide straps that hold his hair from his face. His eyes are light blue, attesting to his mother's people the Ordovikeh and his wife's people, the Kruithne[22]. His pale skin writhes with the movements of tattoos and scarification, and the skin crinkles near his eyes for he is quick to laugh.

His rites of initiation were five years ago and though he has laid with many women it is only now the druids have agreed to an alliance.

His principle wife is Aoife[23], as fair as he is dark, whose forehead is shaved from ear to ear in the tradition of the seers and druids of Inish Môn and who originally came from the battle island, Skye, where legend has it an ancestor of hers, a woman named Scáthach, trained Ku Hulainn and beat him

---

[22] Pronounced Croonyeh

[23] Pron. *Eefa*. She is a product of my imagination because, it must be remembered, (and that most of what we know comes to us from Tacitus) women were hardly mentioned. Unless strategic they were of no account.

again and again, until he learned from her to be great—the greatest warrior of all time, so they say. Aoife is very fertile, earning her much gold, many head of cattle and an abundance of torques. Within three years, she is delivered of three healthy sons.

Caradoc, ap Kymbelineh is the eldest son, now sixteen years old, two years an initiated man, warrior-trained with several kill-feathers all banded in blue for the slaughter of those who would raid his tuath of their cattle. He is handsome, proud and utterly noble, heir to the vast Katuvallunneh territories.

The second son is Tohadumnesh, now fourteen, full of laughter and horny as the bull he guards. The youngest is twelve, Adminish. He walks with a pronounced limp and his face is scarred. He was trampled when the wild horses were brought in several years ago. He has pride in that scar, and he does not care about the jibes from his brothers. The eldest are as dark as their father, but Adminish' hair is stag-red, not surprising really, for he has the look of his mother's people.

Some say that his difference is why he does what he does later.

Kymbelineh is used to power. He is also, by now, quite Rome-friendly, hedging his bets both ways, enjoying the indulgences his back-slapping provides. Tohadumnesh and Caradoc, however, are very aware of the seduction and potential decimation of our ancestral culture and lands.

So, Caradoc trains to one day become chieftain. The man who will, ultimately, unite the priteni people against Rome. He and Budekeh[24]. More on her deeds in good time.

Kymbelineh's brother Ebatekesh is also a warrior and chieftain. He, and a vast band of Katuvallunneh, invade the Atrebatesh, around 20CE, in a land grab.

---
[24] *bánríon* (Keltic: woman *chieftain*) of the Ekeneh people

After savage fighting Ebatekesh gains control. He continues to expand into the Atrebatesh' territory for fifteen years. Until he dies.

Caradoc, aged nineteen, inherits the title of chieftain of the Atrebatesh. What does he do? He hands power back to them. Into the hands of a man named Verikeh who is proclaimed chieftain. Why did Caradoc do this? By now Togh and many other tribal confederacies understand utterly what Rome is doing. Caradoc does not realize his mistake until it is too late.

Caradoc marries. She is Gwynyth[25] of the snow-white hair, young queen of the Silures. They are paired because the druids tell us the portents hint at the necessity of this confederacy. She is his first 'wife'[26]

---

[25] I have invented her because Tacitus only writes of men, with the exception of Budekeh. She existed, whatever her name, because of what happens at the battle of Caer Caradoc in the future.

[26] The terms husband and wife are understood differently in modern culture. I have used them here because there is no known substitute.

and he is her first 'husband[27]'. Under Brehon Law men and women alike can have ten unions, although it is unheard of and seems to me not worth the complication. Caradoc ap Kymbelineh agrees to this first marriage[28], as does Gwynyth of the Shiluresh.

Within a year he and Gwynyth have a daughter. Heir to the Katuvallunneh *rīgjo*[29] after Caradoc, should his brothers not survive him. Gwynyth of the snow-white hair, names her daughter Gwyn[30], for it means white, and mothers often name their children after themselves or their own ancestors.

She trains Gwyn in the ways of weapons and strategy, defense, weather, star and tracking and magic from the time she leaves the breast. Gwyn inherits her first hound and her first horse and is within the saddle by the time she is three. By five she memorizes her familial lineages in case the dreams come to call her

---

[27] ditto
[28] A first-degree union takes place between partners of equal rank and property.
[29] Proto-Keltic: kingdom
[30] Made her up. Named for her mother

to the misty isle and the ways of the druids. She learns by rote the legends of her people and is given carved wooden animals, fish and birds, totems of her clan.

She is adorned in amber and gold. Her hair is not cut. She receives her first kill-feather—silver heron—for trapping a rabbit and cutting its throat all on her own. The feather is woven into her hair, its quill dyed bright red, striking against her paleness. She is six. Her younger brother, Ku[31], born the year after his sister, is trained the same.

Caradoc and his brothers perfect the Roman language. Does Tohadumnesh get a wife? He's such a horny man and women love him. He has lover after lover and sires many children. All known to him. All loved and admired for their prowess at three and four and six and ten. But no wife. I think the druids know him

---

[31] Made him up, as well. Sources do not give either his wife of his children identities. Ku is named for the hound, a variation of his grandfather's name, but Welsh, the land of his mother and his birth.

very well. He prefers to ride horses, and hunt, and dream prophesies.

Adminish, many years later, and a very serious man, is given control of the territory of the Kenteh. Somewhere in all this he becomes confused. Is seduced by Roman ideals of the idea of an empire. Is that it? He turns against the druids and takes his own choice of wife: the daughter of a Roman who lives among the Trinovanteh. It is confusing, but what is certain is that he becomes deeply allied to Rome and therefore, like Mandubrakesh before him, is considered a traitor, banished by his father.

In 40CE Adminish, also like Mandubrakesh before him, cedes to the protection Rome. To Caligula who plans to attack us in his future, but... *"Caligula treated this as if the entire island had submitted to him. Caligula prepared an invasion of Britain, but abandoned it in farcical circumstances, ordering his soldiers to attack the waves and gather seashells as the spoils of victory.*"³²

EKENEH (CALLED ICENI/ECINI)

North of both Katuvallunneh and Trinovanteh tribal lands is the Ekenach. Coastal people. Marsh people and people of the horse and the black river. Their leaders have always been on friendly terms with Rome and have grown fat and wealthy through trade. One or two *rí tuaithe*—chieftains—are pleased to condescend to neighboring tribes by way of Roman privilege and entitlement.

Does everyone in Ekeneh territory consider themselves blessed? It seems not, although recorded history, at this time, does not show us much at all. Two rival chieftains[33] vie for power but do not succeed. But how much the price of submission?

Rome does what it wants. Cruelty, seduction,

---

[32] Suetonius *Lives of the Twelve Caesars: Caligula 44:2-47*

[33] Aesunnos and Saenuvax

extortion, rapid and unprecedented development, exorbitant taxation, coercion and bribery, indulgent trade.

It occupies.

It builds and builds.

Temples, fortresses, alliances, roads, bridges. In the year 47CE an Ekeneh uprising against this tyrannical rule fails in bloodshed. Scapulous installs Prasutagus as king, following the execution of any other contenders. The Ekeneh become a client kingdom.

But this is just the beginning. The real tragedy is still to come.

CHAPTER FIVE
Betrayal

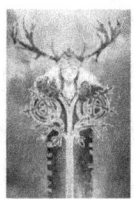

EMPEROR CLAUDIUS DINES ON THE CELTIC SOUL VERIKEH.

The year is 40CE and I begin this section of our story with this man.

Every now and then, in our personal lives and in history as we know it, there comes a turning point. A game changer. Verikeh is such.

Without knowledge of the Katuvallunneh, and over many years, Verikeh is seduced by Roman businessmen. He is flattered and promised great wealth. He agrees to the empire's taxes and terms. And so it is, he is established as a 'client king' creating trade and diplomatic links with Rome, agreeing to anything Rome desires, in return for luxury and protection.

Because of Verikeh, the Atrebateh territories are now divided, so the Katuvallunneh take control of several duns and many miles of forest and fen to the south of their own lands. And again, because of this, and to protect our livelihood from further decay, Caradoc takes control of both his own people's interests and those of the Atrebatesh.

Bear in mind, and I must admit, the Katuvallunneh have had it both ways for decades. They have traded back and forth with many other countries, including Rome, and Caradoc's grandfather, Taskyavanesh was used to his pleasures, as was his father. It is country they refuse to relinquish, and the ways of the priteni people. They enjoy wealth and always have. I must say I'm not surprised of Verikeh's envy, of just how far he was prepared to go to get what Kymbelineh and the other *rí tuaithe* have.

Verikeh acts to the detriment of the people, savage and demanding, breaking cultural laws. A despot puppet. The druids and the Brehons will not allow this to continue, and. his spies inform him that his execution is at hand. His life depends on him leaving, and he flees.

Verikeh is granted asylum in Rome.

What does he do? He grovels before the current emperor Claudius, begging for an army to retake his kingdom. Reminding said emperor of our wild, green lands, and that all of them are not yet his.

Claudius agrees.

CLAUDIUS, EMPEROR

We need to know a little of Claudius because it is during his reign, and because of his decisions, his orders and his military, that the lights and the souls of the p/briteneh people are almost extinguished.

He's a sad little man, really. Born in Gaul, not Rome, he is ostracized early in life due to a stutter, a limp, hearing impairment, a shaking head, a tendency to slobber and his knees to occasionally give way beneath him. All caused by childhood illness[34]. He is known for his rages. He is known for enjoying brutal gladiatorial events and has married four times. He has had to share his consulship with Caligula (who is mad and who is subsequently assassinated). Claudius is also paranoid. Called pathetic, dull and easily influenced.

And here, because of Verikeh, he is presented with the opportunity of a lifetime. Take over an entire land belonging to somebody else.

Rome should have realized, a hundred years ago that we have spies everywhere. Relays. Sentries. In Rome two hundred, three hundred, pretend and listen. Particularly now. And Claudius likes to mingle with

---

[34] Some have thought cerebral palsy, others early childhood polio, others Tourette Syndrome

simple men.

THE THIRD INVASION (CLAUDIUS)

43CE. Winter. A season of heavy snow. Travel between nations is treacherous. If communities have not stockpiled sufficiently during harvest they will starve. Only those 'client kingdoms' under Roman occupation prosper. The Kelts are now divided.

Four legions[35] and twenty thousand auxiliaries, including Thracians and Batavians, sail towards the coast in three divisions.

They weigh anchor, and forge to land at the same beachhead as Caesar, the now-Romanized Kentax territory. They make shore under the control of the general Aulus Plautius. Future emperor Vespasian taking lead of the first landing. Titus Flavius Sabinus (the son, not the father), his brother, also here to document events while Claudius demands fealty to

---

[35] Approximately 24,000 people, in this case IX Hispania, XIV Gemina, XX Valeria Victis and II Augusta

Rome or suffer the consequences.

They initially meet no resistance.

The army assembles a temporary fort, dig latrines, kill and cook livestock brought with them from Gaul, create elaborate dining and sleeping quarters for Claudius' elite, and settle in for the night.

Claudius, Platius, Vespasian and Verikeh keep as warm as possible, against the sea-mist and silently falling snow. In the forests beyond the beachhead are the ghosts of the unquiet dead.

This place evokes fear. It is not lit as is Rome. No roads, no wide spaces for vineyard or lanes of tame and entertaining poplars. Just endless forest, moaning. Fog, the scream of vixen in season, the whoosh of owl wing and the unexpected raven strike when shouldn't they be sleeping? And then, as though to drive them crazy, the relentlessness, incessant roar of the sea.

Sentries sense the presences of these malevolent ancestral ghosts. Everywhere, just beyond the stony beach. The soldiers ride back and forth, back and forth, along the perimeter of the encampment, bristling with weapons, their breath white, their pupils dilated.

Within sturdy tents braziers warm the night. Low couches. Light. And Claudius, Platius, Vespasian and Verikeh drink copious quantities of wine, and dine at an elaborate table before bedding the comfort women that are always brought on such campaigns. Claudius is a known womanizer.

The following day everything is taken down again, and the invaders forge inland...

… And that is where we wait. On the plain between the rivers Medway and Tamesha (Thames). Caradoc and Tohadumnesh ride gaily bedecked horses, alongside dozens of loyal chieftains from the tribal alliances.

They thunder up and down before the ranks of seventeen thousand amassed warriors. Women, men, children old enough and strong enough to fight, druids, bards, dreamers, musicians. Our breath frosting the white day, the horses whuffling, stamping. Our hound excited. The weather not a bother.

We are dressed for this event, in wolf skin and fox hide, finely tanned leather, with kill feathers and threads of gold wound into our hair. Our bodies are warm with animal fat, arms and necks adorned with the torques that represent us. White clay, red ochre, the colors of ash and sky, whorled and webbed tattoos of our initiations and ancestral stories, black hair and grey, red and fair as this snow. Earrings, gold and carnelian, crafted at home or from as far away as Egypt and India, glinting through the early morning mists that the Romans do not understand and so despise.

Druids in blackbird and raven capes, their hair clayed

into serpents. Men and the shadow-women, their talismans and weapons, weather magic and whispered invocations and enchantments ready to paralyze. We have decorated our spears, javelins, swords in sheaths of leather and bronze, bound about with iron, knives in our belts and scabbards about our shoulders, shields of bull hide, wood, painted with the sigils of tribal spirits and totems, wind and water. Hawk and eagle-guardians, the birds of prey mounted on hard leather greaves, as much an enemy to our enemy as hound and horse and hunter.

We are seventeen thousand. We should number twenty times that, or a million. But no. We have called on the people, but only those not yet surrendered, only they have come. The Silures and Ordovikeh from the mountains to the west are here, the Dumnonach and Durratrijah from the south, from the lands of tin, trade, the white cliffs and the plains of the great henge. Even the wildest of us all—the Kalledonach —ride dressed in great furs. Every able druid from Inish Môn, the Brehons from across the western sea. And us, the indestructible Brijanax from the north. We are four thousand.

Word arrives that the Dobunneh to the west have surrendered to the now Romanized Katuvallunneh. The spies do not know why. We had wondered at their failure to show.

BATTLE

And here they come. The great fucking Roman Empire. Pennants atop high spears, gold ensigns and standards bearing the eagle as though it were theirs alone, alike in galea, greaves and lorica, short tunics as well as bracccae. Some wear the coolus helmet, some the imperial. Lots of red and the pretense of gold. All with swords or pila, shields, ranks bearing sagittarii.

Then... what is that? What on earth are those? Caradoc? Togh?

The huge grey beasts lumber from the ships and up the beach, wicker baskets strapped onto their backs loaded with soldiers, bedecked with finery, silks of many colors bronze, leather, purple and scarlet saddles. Armor of hardened leather.

They're war elephants, says Caradoc quietly. Tohadumnesh stands in the saddle to one side of his brother, the better to see the show, while Gwynyth at his other sits calmly upon the night-black mare. Oh, she answers, as though she already knew, glancing back to where her children laugh and flirt with other warriors, anticipating the kill-feathers and bravery they will achieve today.

The elephants take to the front lines.

There he is. Caradoc gestures, and spits. Claudius the idiot. The monster. He rides atop the lead elephant in all his splendor. How I hate him and his audacity. How I hate Verekeh who sits astride a Roman horse, attired as a Roman, bearing Roman weapons. Traitor.

What have you done all in the name of greed? The heritage you have rejected? How your ancestors must keen upon the wind at the sight of you. The smell of you, stinking of Roman perfume. How did you come to this? How low. You would betray your own people for baubles and soft cloth? We will remember you, Verica. You will be the first to die today.

But he does not. The coward says something to the man astride the big bay beside him, then turns about and rides to the rear of the auxiliary. I cannot see him anymore.
How many, Togh? How many, I overhear.
Too many, whispers Caradoc, to only Togh.

The first day is a bloodbath, savage, slaughter. It is madness. We are outmatched. Outnumbered. Limbs and broken people everywhere, the ravens already feasting. They are the first of the other kin on the scene to slake their hunger on the corpses of the slain and so take us to the next life. We withdraw but we will not run. We roar, and weep, and sleep badly and awake before dawn. Readying ourselves. We live and die. We are not cowed. Until the battle today. Five thousand of us murdered, and hardly a Roman harmed.

We leave. We ride west, many going into fever, their wounds to gangrene along the way to safety. We cannot bring our dead, but they are earth and air, wind and rain and food for many generations. They will be our descendants. Caradoc and Arica the druid support Tohadumnesh. We fear he is mortally wounded, and we don't know if he will make it to the stronghold, let alone through the night. His arm is almost severed, and an arrow has punctured a lung. He fights to breathe and spits blood.

The Romans do not follow. They don't cheer as we leave the plain and because of their lack of manners we spit on their memory. They should have roared their honor of the day and the dead.

Tohadumnesh dies tonight.

LEY LINES AND CONFEDERATE ALLIANCES

By now the tribes of the south and east: the Catuvellauni, the Trinovanteh, the Kenteh, just south, and the Atrebatesh, are all subdued. That ham-fisted thug Ostorius Scapulus declares that he intends to disarm us. All of us. Subdued or otherwise. Can he be serious? How?

No, says Caradoc. We gather as one people. We defy them.

We dissolve into the year-round mist-veiled mountainous terrain, and the deep hidden valleys who are the Shiluresh and Ordovikeh, in the west.

Over the ensuing weeks and months many thousands join us. Too many for the game and livestock in this part of the country. For the next four years Mona feeds us. They grow abundant grain, and trade with the Kalledonax for meat, but we have learned to eat bread as a staple, instead of boar.

The Romans do not know, or they would torch the land and poison the water.

The territories to the east *are* disarmed, except for what is required to hunt and farm the now timid lands. The Ekeneh are disarmed. How is the Budekeh going to deal with that? She won't deal with it. What will she do?

CHAPTER FOUR

47CE – EKENEH, TRIBE OF THE RUIRÍ, CALLED THE BUDEKEH

We are the Ekeneh. We are the country and ocean to the east, where sun and moon and stars rise from the sea. We are the river, the marsh, the chariot and the horse. We were not involved in the Claudian invasion, instead succumbing to Rome in a mainly peaceful treaty, agreeing to their terms for tax and trade. It seems easier to join the surrounding provinces also thus aligned. As such we prosper and are not harmed. That is in stark difference to the inland tribes whom we hardly ever see. Many of our chieftains and their families have, however, defected and have gone west to join the guerrilla confederacy. Claudius appoints Antedewush, as a *client regent.*

Once he was a proud and adept chieftain, but Rome abducted his daughter, raped her, took her and many others to Rome and refused their return unless Antedewush subject his territories to their demands. We are warriors, and a people of the horse, but for many decades our main trade has been barley and wheat. The soil is rich and alluvial, the crops abundant. We have known many years of peace the intruder does not bother us.

Until the demand for disarmament, that is. No. Not so. We will not lie on our backs and we will not allow our enemies that flight of fancy. So, no. We mobilize. We prepare our defenses.

Ostorius sets the legions against us at the fortress of Shtoneh. We are the first tribe to take a stand against this ridiculous demand, but are very soon joined by warriors from territories surrounding us.

Antedewush refuses to join us, so it is Brashetahesh, Budekeh's consort and *ruirí* who leads us. He is a bull of a man, but he moves with the fluid grace of a runner. He has traveled much in his lifetime and that is all of twenty three years. His light brown hair hangs loose, and he is banded about his forehead with stranded wire of gold and bronze made for him at the time of his manhood. His sword is iron and comes from the north, inscribed with sigils of protection and courage. He wears it on his back, over the finely worked otter skins but under the bear cloak. He is a man of few words and loves Budekeh and his two daughters more than his own life. And I can see why.

She is of the Kalledonax on her mother's side and Inish Môn on her father's. She grew up on that island. Became druid. She has inherited the forest[36] of her ancestors, the one with the depthless spring that leads to the heart of the world. That is huge. That is an entire free-standing forest. She is tall and muscular from wielding her mother's sword; her hair is as red

---

[36] Now known as Thetford, and in the modern world sporting only pine trees, it was the original fortress forest of the Ekeneh people.

as the pelt of the summer fox.

She laughs much, and is kind to her slaves. Covered from head to toe in the torques and jewelry showered upon her by Brashetahesh she is a chieftain in her own right, training alongside the other warriors, summer and winter. Her tattoos display an ancestral connection to many other clans. She is a force to be reckoned with for there are few who do not claim her as their true chieftain.

It is coming on winter and we do not have time to rebuild our stronghold. The place we have chosen to stand against the arrogance of Claudius is difficult to access. We have that in our favor and Rome's cavalry contingents cannot get to us. Ostorius has his legionaries come upon us on foot.

The fighting is fierce. Day after day, for almost four days. But the vulnerability of our fortifications is our undoing. We are beaten.

Brashetahesh remained at the forefront of the battle but was brought down, his horse speared. He was surrounded by seven well-armed legionaries. They would want to take him prisoner, an example to the rest of us, but he will not come, his sword scything at them as he turns in circles. Ekeneh warriors rally, Budekeh's war cry ululating over the heads of pitched battle. They drive the enemy from Brashetahesh but not before he takes a deadly slash to his sword arm that almost severs it above the elbow.

By the time the battle is over, and we are beaten, infection has set into his wound.

Go home, yells Ostorius, from the safety of distance. *Behave yourselves. You cannot win. Now disarm.*

Brashetahesh's arm is amputated. The healers do all they can and so saved his life. But the wound suppurates no matter what. It does not heal. It will never heal and within a few years it will kill him.

We are seen to disarm. It is a ruse. Prasutagus pushes Antedewush for our rights to individuation but no. We are sick of you, Antedewesh. You agree to whatever Claudius desires.

We do not. Go ahead, immortalize yourself on golden coins. I am no seer, but I know this: in generations to come your name will hardly matter. Your daughter would fall on her sword if she knew what you have become.

Antedewush conveniently dies from some 'unknown ague' not many months after, when some shadowed hero slips a few *death caps*[37] into his venison stew. He is replaced, as *regi*, by Brashetahesh, by now very certain of the ley of things. He knows that Rome is ruthless behind that sweet, placating demeanor. It is here to take, and he must do what he can to protect not only his family but the people. He knows that the title of banruirí should be Budekeh's but, with only

---

[37] Mushroom/fungi – species: Amanita phalloides

ever one exception—that of Kartimandweh to the wild and unresolved north—women hold no power in the eyes of Rome.

Budekeh bristles.

They fight between themselves. What has he done to shut her up? To avoid the insurrection, she so dearly wants? It is never known. Keep our daughters safe, perhaps he asks? How, she would have replied, when they have left us as vulnerable as kittens? She agrees... for whatever reason. Rome has said, in return, that the Ekeneh shall retain their sovereignty, their wealth and their established safety. They have signed a treaty of agreement.

The Ekeneh, during the Roman occupation, remained relatively independent, in difference to the Trinovanteh tribe and territory that was decimated for what he invaders considers sedition. While he lived, and before the uprising, Brashetahesh proclaimed Rome his co-beneficiaries, alongside his two daughters, in his death wishes, witness by Brehon druids and therefore beyond dispute. He was not really supposed to set anything aside for his offspring.

We have an agreement with Rome, Brashetahesh announces at the tribal gathering at the time of the spring thaw just before the planting. Does it mean anything, Budekeh, hisses into his ear? Rome lied.

In the heart of the Trinovanteh lands, now overtaken by the Kashuvalluneh, at the same time, the building of a vast fortress and Roman city has begun. It is constructed quickly, as at this Rome is brilliant, and it is built well. It is the capital of Rome in priteni people's lands, and its name is Kamulodden. It is built on an ancient Keltic fortress[38] older than the known world. The Romans equate it to their god of war, although how they come to that conclusion is a matter of misunderstanding.

---

[38] Pitchbury Ramparts, considered the most extensive iron age fortifications in of the Priteni.

CHAPTER SEVEN
CARADOC

50CE – WALES

We continue to train for war, and to come and go almost normally (if not guardedly). We trade, marry, welcome bards from across the sea. Egyptians, Hellenes, Scythian philosophers trading wisdom for wisdom, horses for horses and gold for golden eagles, all the way from the Steppes and the Altai mountains.

Children are born. New seers come of age and are guided to Mona to learn the secrets of the shadowy way, to take initiations. Spies travel the land, whispering to the mists and heeding their replies. We have many council meetings to think about, consider, and discuss the Roman ways of fighting. We must. To outsmart them. Near forty thousand have broken away from every tribe to join us.

The Romans build a fortress in a day. We burn it down. Never a battle, always a skirmish. Fight and fight and run away, live to fight another day.

Caradoc now bears razor-thin cuts in three clean lines, on both his cheeks, a blood offering for the success of the raid they are about to make upon the new garrison being built not forty miles from the lowlands.

He and many others have rubbed their wounds with the ash from the fires of twenty sacred boughs the druids burned in their honor. So that now the thin grey lines form a new story, his resolve another peril that Rome has to endure. The warriors burn that fortress to the ground.

Budekeh comes in stealth and remains a week. She stays in the dun with Caradoc. What do they discuss? It isn't known, and it isn't shared. What we do know is that she has promised Brashetahesh that she will not rise up against Rome while he lives. From what I have gleaned that may not be long.

At the same time Claudius' representatives Aulus Platius, Scapulus, Geta and Saturninus attempt to forge inland. They invade aggressively. As far as they can. Scorched earth. They take what crops, cattle they need and burn the rest so that the people are too hungry for dissension. They attack and decimate the Dekanjeleh tribe that lives on the lowlands to the north east of the Ordovikesh. They take the land at what is called Cheshire Gap, in the tribal territories of the Brijanteh.

The Brijanteh leader, once *wosaljaxto, is now a traitor—regina*—Kartimandweh[39], when still a young greedy woman, bloodlessly agreed that these lands to the wild—and to strangers inhospitable—north has become a *client civitate* for the gain of Rome's many

---

[39] Reigned from 43 to 69. May have been one of the 11 'kings' who Claudius trumpeted gave in without a fight.

promised pleasures aimed at her personally. How can this happen? It's occurring more and more. It is many years since she was first, and secretly, seduced by silk, perfume, pretty male slaves, delicacies Rome has showered upon her. The traitor welcomes—or at least is not seen to object—to garrisons and fortresses being built and colonized in our territories. This offensive effectively creates a barrier; a wedge, between north and south. It is not known how deeply she has become enthralled. Caradoc doesn't know.

The midland tribes have joined us now. We are heavily armed. Well organized. Guerrilla warriors. Our spies are everywhere. Rome does not know the ways of Keltic women and children.

But then, by the year that will, when you rea this, be known as 50 CE, it all becomes too much. Too many lives lost, innocents murdered, raped, Roman children born into tribes that don't want them but that can't reject them (that's the big story). Homes burned, cattle pillaged, crops destroyed. Starvation ravages the clans, the territories to the east vanquished, already Roman. Weak with alien-seeming wealth. Enough is enough. Caradoc and the many chieftains allied to them, the Ordovikeh, Shiluresh, druids, those of the old ways, tribal ways amass by the thousands, to put an end to it.

BATTLE OF CAER CARADOC

Over many days we prepare. Gather close to the hill fortress. Druids seek omens from the shapes of flights of birds, from the way the wind whispers. Gaining promises from the spirits of the ancient dead, promising to stand with us. To unnerve the enemy from the twilight gate, that potent place of magic between the day and the night. Of course, they whisper to any able to hear them. We are great and we are still here. It was they who raised the standing stones and the long barrows just miles from here. For this is Caersŵs. And shall, for ever more, also be Caer Caradoc.

We camp close by with our families. Gwynyth covered in ash, her hair white with lime, tied up with ribbons of rabbit fur to resemble the tail of her horse, her totems a blur of whorls across her cheeks, the skins on wolves upon her shoulders and down her back, her naked body glistening with grease, polishing her swords, plaiting white owl feathers into her daughter's snow-white hair, watching her sixteen year old son prepare both of their weapons. They will fight. All who can, will fight. The elders, the children, the newly initiated. The singers with the power to raise the mists. The dreamers that remember the legends and manifest their representatives. The druids from Inis Môn. Their bards whose memories are as long as the sea is wide.

We have armed the slaves and they bristle with the anticipation of promised freedom. We have cut the throats of the hostages. We have beasts for slaughter, butchers, cooks, blacksmiths, handlers of the horses and the hounds. Swords and daggers sharpened. Slings and stones. Hawks without their hunting jesses. Great fires hardening the tips of newly made javelins and spears. Fortifications to the slopes are rebuilt and enhanced. The horses are ready. The hounds, fighting amongst themselves in the heat of testosterone-fueled energy, bristle and strut.

This time it is not in customary vanity that we lime and dress our hair, oil our bodies, adorn them with amber and jet, gold and bronze, talismans, the heads of our ancestors hung from the poles supporting cover. No. This is to remind each other that we are the people. This is our culture. These lands are us and we will not be overcome even if we are killed to the last because we will become the earth upon which we die. Be every bird and boar and bear and other brother and sister that feeds upon us, or the grass and trees and fungi that grow from where we are slain.

Caersŵs. High enough to see in all directions. An ancient dun. Fortified. The empire of Rome wants the west, the northwest, the north. Where they thus have not subdued. *We cannot let them. Fuck them.* The spirit of the river sings to us in the night, the light rain a kiss, ravens storytelling through the mist in the morning.

At dawn, the sun limns the eastern horizon. And there they are, the vast smudge of them marring the horizon. In excess of twenty one thousand under the banners of Publius Ostorius Scapula and his fucking golden eagle.

Our camp is dismantled and all who will not fight return to the safety of the territory of the Ordovikesh where the Romans cannot go.

CHAPTER EIGHT

A Cruelty of Fate

THE TRAGEDY OF WAR

Spears and javelins like rain. But the enemy is not killed. Testudo after testudo[40] they dismantle the fortress stones and swarm. Hour upon hour. Too many. They do not die this day. We do. We must retreat to yet another hill. The legionaries pursue. The auxiliaries attack from the rear. Everyone fights how they can. Friend cannot see friend, mother cannot see daughter. Confusion. Tripping over the dead and dying, blood in our eyes clouding vision. Screams. I hear screams as people are taken. They would rather die here. At the end of the day we must run. All who

---

[40] From the Latin *tortoise*: shield protection above and around

can, escape. We run, take to our horses, the hounds following, the hawks screaming from the dirty sky.

It is night. We have made it back to the black hills. We hunt for our loved ones. We wait to see who will live beyond the night. Caradoc searches, but Gwynyth and their children are not here. Are they dead?

He keens in mourning, for what else could have happened? If they are not slain upon the battlefield he will find them. If Rome has taken them prisoner, they will know who they have. They have killed the children. Men and women, warriors of the people, lie in pools of blackened blood, their eyes open, their bodies hacked to pieces.

A messenger arrives. Gwynyth and Caradoc's children are captive. Hostage. Platius says, you want them? Alive? Come and meet me. Give yourself up. Or they will be taken to Rome as trophies of war.

More. We need more warriors. Come on! We can still

win this.

Caradoc rides, that night, to the stronghold of the Kartimandweh.
Please, he begs.
Relax, she says. *Stay while I work out the logistics.*
Can I trust you?
She laughs and says *of course,* and sets her servants to laying a great feast in honor of her guest and his retinue. No, explains Caradoc. I'm tired. We just want to sleep. Oh, of course. I understand, she says, her look compassionate.

He is woken, hammered as some blunt force weapon slams into the side of his head. He rolls, reaches for his weapons, they are gone. He is beaten to a pulp, chained and imprisoned along with his company.

The Romans come for them the next day. Kartimandweh, *regina* of the Brijanteh, is paid exorbitantly for this treasure.

Caradoc is taken to Rome, as a prize of war and a sacrifice to Mithra. *Look! We have captured a barbarian king! What a prize. What an ugly, hairy man.*

Initially Caradoc is paraded in a bear cage. It is intended that he be ceremonially executed as part of a triumphal parade. But he is brought before the senate and asked to speak. And stuns them with his grasp of their language and the eloquence of his words.

Tacitus records his account:

If the degree of my nobility and fortune had been matched by moderation in success, I would have come to this city as a friend rather than a captive, nor would you have disdained to receive with a treaty of peace one sprung from brilliant ancestors and commanding a great many nations. But my present lot, disfiguring as it is for me, is magnificent for you. I had horses, men, arms, and wealth: what wonder if I was unwilling to lose them? If you wish to command everyone, does it really follow that everyone should accept your slavery? If I were now being handed over as one who had surrendered immediately, neither my fortune nor your glory would have achieved brilliance. It is also true that in my case any reprisal will be followed by oblivion.[41]

They free him. And Gwynyth and their children are there. But none will ever return to their own lands, will never be permitted. That is the saddest cut of all. Caradoc dies within a short time of his exile.

We never know what becomes of Gwynyth and their children. In secret I hope they have escaped and will return to us one day, triumphant. His ancestors are still here, though. I would ask you to know that.

Claudius, beside himself at his own achievements, then leads his military and all his followers to the city of Kamuloddun and summons the chieftains of his eleven client colonies, called by the Anglo-Saxon

---

[41] Tacitus *Annals*, 12.37

word *kings*, whose names are to be inscribed, for all time, on his yet-to-be-erected British Victory Arch in Rome. The list is known to have included Antedwesh, of the Ekeneh, posthumously.

AND WHAT OF CLAUDIUS?

Claudius then returns to Rome. Two years later, in 54, he is murdered with poison, and replaced by the next madman (perhaps even responsible for the assassination), Claudius' nephew, Nero. He declared that Claudius was actually a god. He had a temple built in Kamulodden, renamed *Camulodinum* in his honor.

The chieftains are supposed to go there once a year to worship him.

PART THREE

CHAPTER NINE

THE DRUID ISLE

58CE –

Around the time of Prasutagus death Caius Suetonius Paullinus, a general as nasty as Ostorius, but unfortunately more savvy, is appointed governor of all the lands of the Priteni, told by the emperor to find and execute insurgents. He wants Kymru[42] and, eventually the entire north, the perennial homeland of the Kalledoneh. But we have been here for over twenty nine thousand years. Our lands are not for some

---

[42] Originally meaning 'those of us', not a place name at all, it was the mountainous territory to the far north west that after subsequent invasions was known by the Anglo-Saxon word Wales

stranger's taking. We know and honor every hill and copse of father yew. The rowan to the south has guarded all within her reign for a thousand years. Our offensive prevents the occupation of north, west and south. But they cannot get us. How could they stop us?

These year-round, mist-shrouded mountains, with snow on the highest peaks are as alien to them as their elephants are to us.

Paullinus has found out who feeds us.

MONA

Geese in flight at the wrong time of year, And at dawn? Wake up! Wake up! They are coming! Seers jerking from trance to wakefulness. Clouds ominous, warning us. Prepare. They are almost upon us. Dip the torches in pitch. Light them. Dress the women as shadows and night. Hide the raven cloak and the owl masks. Wrap them in leather and bury them deep within the forest. Take the children, too young to fight, to safety. No one is too old to fight. Arm yourselves.

There they are. Dear brother bear, how many?

"It has been said to have been one of the bloodiest campaigns undertaken by the Romans in Britain, acknowledging that the purpose of the campaign and its leader – Suetonius Paullinus – were both well matched. In reality there were only ever two ways in which to bring other civilisations under the pax Romana; assimilation within the Roman way – or annihilation...

"Killing an enemy who has run away is easier than killing one that stands to fight – and the Romans exploited this weakness to the full.

It is said that they spared none they met on that bloody field of battle. Men, women and children were slaughtered, butchered by an army spurred on by its earlier shame. Many of the Druids and their followers were thrown into their sacred groves of oak and then burned alive. There were, it is said, few prisoners taken..."

Then...

"Today, the bloody shore runs from Moel-y-Don to the sou'west of Llanfair PG to Tal-y-Foel opposite Caernarfon. Even today, the shore bears testimony to the carnage of that day's events. Place names such as Bryn-y-Beddau, the Hill of Graves, still appear on modern maps of the island. Here the islanders who survived after Paullinus had left to fight Boudicca buried their dead. Above the village of Llanidan, are two fields still known as The Field of the Long Battle and the Field of Bitter Lamentation. There is also Plas Goch, the Red Place; its name giving a hint to the story behind it." [43]

---

[43] *The Roman Invasion of Anglesey*, John Griffiths
http://www.militaryhistoryonline.com/ancient/anglesey/
Contacted for permission to quote, Midwinter Solstice 2015. No reply.

Tacitus' account of what, in the distant future, will be known as the *Menai Massacre* does not state the numbers slaughtered on this day. That Rome sets up camp on that far west coast is clear. That the soldiers are afraid of the magic of the druids is also clear. That Mona is refuge to many thousands of warriors in hiding from the Roman occupation is also well known. But not the numbers.

I can't write this. How can I keep writing this? The story is not changing. We are not winning. This is genocide. No one could conceive of such a thing. Rome wants it all. Everywhere we turn our homelands are being confiscated. Stolen. Our identities and our culture, has avalanched from within the mists of forever, has brought the cattle from the high country every spring and has suckled the hound pup at the breast of one of us when its own mother could not. If we die your own children will not know who you have been. Who you once were, who you are still but do not know it. What is that but homelessness? Are we to be obliterated?

So that day there was also slaughter and bloodshed because although we are warriors we are not, and never could be, mindless soldiers.

Their capacity for violation and cruelty is staggering. We are nothing to them. They rape us. They burn our brother and sister trees until we are ashes. Our brother and sister of every species, cremated ruthlessly.

From the other side of the water we watch as hour upon hour they keep coming. By the thousand. As efficient as ants. Their horses pulling giant ballistae, catapults capable of hurling flame or iron or pouches of heavy stone, and onagers, smaller of the same. They set up a vast camp. Dozens upon dozens of flat-bottomed water craft messing up the foreshore of the Menai. We ride our chariots up and down the beach screaming curses, summoning wild weather to drown them, blind them, sweep them out to sea. We bang our spears and swords against our shields in a deafening thunder. The shadow-mothers summon up the ghosts of our ancestors to drive the enemy mad.

And then that fiery rain comes. Fire. From those wicked contraptions. Our priority is to protect the tuath, the forest, our livelihood. So many now caught up in dousing the conflagration.

Then the boats. Oh, we sink many, don't think we do not. The ocean works with us to rip them away. But they keep coming. Cavalry ride wildly swimming horses, some men beside their beasts pulling them with a will. The tide is shallow, you see. They come as a swarm. Wasps. Intent on our destruction. How did they know? We are the backbone of the body. The heart. The lungs and the fire in the head. I see Seutonius Paullinus in his own chariot. Looks like gold. His standard is, that's certain. He does not come. He makes small gestures to centurions left and right. From these almost delicate hands, men of the highest ranks among them move in arcs and swathes.

Then they are upon us. We fight with every possible butchery. All day. So much blood. So much blood. Then Paullinus comes. When we are slaughtered or running through the forest to escape. We hear it first. What is that noise? Louder. Roaring like I have never heard before. And we run, as swiftly as swallows fly, seeking the secret caves that pock the cliffs that face the wild and raging Irish Sea.

Tacitus states, in his chronicles, *that we druids drench our altars in the blood of others and seek omens in human entrails*. One might wonder at the propaganda in his writing when considering the ritualised murder of the gladiatorial 'games'. Though we need him to record his accounts of history we must remember who he is working for. Because, though we do kill? It's to give. What is "sacrifice" to your mind? Those we kill, by the threefold death, are gifts to the land that are given or taken necessarily. To her wells and lakes. Our forest, dear mother, is burning. All night we hide and listen to her dying.

Paullinus would have torn down every standing stone, broken our initiatory mounds, left no trace if he could have. But there wasn't sufficient time. He received news today, of what we learned at dawn. Now they tear down their camp and the trundle of ballistae dwindle further and further behind the legions that run and ride for Londinium[44]. For Kamuloddun is already burned to the ground while the butcher wraps up here, tickling his ego with our extermination.

---

[44] One hypothesis of the name *London* was developed by Richard Coates of the University of Sussex. Coates argues that *London* came from the pre-Keltic name for the lower part of the Thames River, *Plownonida*. This is Coates suggestion of what the river was called in the pre-Keltic language. Coates based this on Indo-European root words that appeared in names for rivers and features of rivers elsewhere in Europe. The Kelts inhabited the region but the Keltic tongue **but they do not pronounce** *p* so the river became *Lownida* and the settlement *Lownedonjon*. Other explanations regard the use of don as dun (fortress) therefore equating the original name to like *Dublin* deriving from the Keltic for *black (dark) pool*. Dub or dubh is *black*.

PART FOUR

CHAPTER TEN

...the Dying of the Light.
                        Excerpt, Dylan Thomas

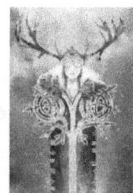

BRINGER OF VICTORY

Dawn. Ravens congregating in a storytelling of perhaps a hundred. What do you say, raven? Budekeh, the *ruirí* of the Ekeneh people, like the final strike of a hammer on the sword, is now ready to move? Budekeh is a title, not a name. It means *victory* (no one recorded her name). She intends to fulfill its meaning. She has raised an army of thousands and rises up against Rome. Is this the pact she made with Caradoc on that silent, secretive foray into Shiluresh' lands?

What? She is burning the cities and fortresses they have built on our ancestral lands? Oh sun and wind and sea, we have a chance now. Surely?

But then we are told why this has happened and it is terrible indeed.

Yes, the so-called treaty Rome offered Brashetahesh was rubbish.

When he died every soldier and his cohort came into Ekeneh territory and took. Budekeh was publicly whipped till the skin hung from her back. Her daughters, aged ten and twelve, were raped. So many rapes. They have driven the traditional owners from their strongholds, off their lands, put to work, banished into exile. Many are dead. Obscenely tortured. All who oppose are sentenced to death for the Roman crime of sedition. Our ancestral possessions are stolen, our people enslaved, our slaves reversing their course.

Here's what she said, for Tacitus, our almost-man on the ground, he seems almost druid-like. Except for the propaganda, of course. Able to be in two places at once:

Suetonius while thus occupied received tidings of the sudden revolt of the province. Prasutagus, king of the Iceni, famed for his long prosperity, had made the emperor his heir along with his two daughters, under the impression that this token of submission would put his kingdom and his house out of the reach of wrong. But the reverse was the result, so much so that his kingdom was plundered by centurions, his house by slaves, as if they were the spoils of war.

First, his wife Boudicea was scourged and his daughters outraged.

All the chief men of the Iceni, as if Rome had received the whole country as a gift, were stripped of their ancestral possessions, and the king's relatives were made slaves. Roused by these insults and the dread of worse, reduced as they now were into the condition of a province, they flew to arms and stirred to revolt the Trinobantes and others who, not yet cowed by slavery, had agreed in secret conspiracy to reclaim their freedom.

It was against the veterans that their hatred was most intense. For these new settlers in the colony of Camulodunum drove people out of their houses, ejected them from their farms, called them captives and slaves, and the lawlessness of the veterans was encouraged by the soldiers, who lived a similar life and hoped for similar licence. [45]

Budekeh allies with the Trinovanteh because, what had been done to them since their submission in the last few years? Again, Tacitus explains:

A temple also erected to the Divine Claudius was ever before their eyes, a citadel, as it seemed, of perpetual

---

[45] Tacitus' *Annals*: Book 14: 31

tyranny. Men chosen as priests had to squander their whole fortunes under the pretence of a religious ceremonial. It appeared too no difficult matter to destroy the colony, undefended as it was by fortifications, a precaution neglected by our generals, while they thought more of what was agreeable than of what was expedient.

This is how you rouse a war. We never did hand over our weapons, even though we seemed to comply. And our smiths continued to hammer and temper sword and shield and dagger, hidden within eaves, beneath barns, in caches at holy places, deep within the briar.

THETFORD FOREST[46]

In *Tacitus Book 14, Chapter 35*, he shares "*Boudica's speech*" to her gathered kindred and allies. These are the *people*. They are of every age. Young enough for

---

[46] Thet: Saxon for *people.* It was the People's Forest. Originally the province of the Sitomajax people (P/Briteni: People of the ford).

this to be their first blood, sufficiently mature to recall the ways of the ancestors, some the first generation since Caesar, so the stories of their elders, and their freedom from tyranny and alien ruin are as fresh in their minds as yesterday. Their scars filled with ash, their kill feathers' quills banded by many colors, each earned, each blessed by the spirit of the kill, the hearth and the high mountain ash. They have good reason to have stayed strong and healthy despite everything forced upon them. They are their own weapons... and ours. They are mainly Trinovanteh and Ekeneh although the news has spread so far and wide that unconquered war bands come from across the entire land.

We gather in secret in the great forest of the Ekeneh heartland. It isn't named Thetford yet. Massive earth ramparts, nearby fortress hill, from which sentries can see in all directions.

Two hundred and thirty thousand warriors, druids, bakers, cooks, eagle-whisperers, bards, lovers, children, gather. It is night, and the wind is up, spreading this news of preparation. The moon full, that face of the hare solemnly watching, illuminating from amongst the vastness of oak and ash, yew and birch, apple, hawthorn, fir, holly and fern. Druids form a ring around the spring, in the heart of this forest, the stronghold of the Ekeneh spirit, cleared of ivy and stinging nettles. Budekeh and her daughters are at that heart. They pull torques from necks and arms. They wordlessly drop them into the bottomless deep. They observe and are pleased. *We will do everything we can*, say the ancestors of every species.

It was only Cassius Dio[47] came up with the idea of a speech and a hare promising victory. What does he know? He is not born for a hundred years. His words suggest someone else, for no druid was given the wrong outcome by any hare. And speeches were a Roman thing. And, as for her *praying to Andrasta*? Maybe. But what I do know is that the word derives from a Roman/Italian one, *andate*, which means the

---

[47] Cassius Dio, Roman History, Book 62, verses 1 – 7

outward journey, so I can understand the misunderstanding.

We have taken the stronghold of Kamuloddun, rightfully, of the Trinovanteh. We have taken the city that Rome has built, and that they call *Londinium*, that dwells on the banks of the great river in the territory of the Katuvallunneh, and we have burned it to the ground.

We take that back, as well. History will tell that we slaughtered in excess of eighty thousand. Who's counting? We move to the next of their settlements, Uerulamium[48], once stronghold of the Katuvallunneh also, and built on the banks of the river Uer. We destroy it and the colonists within it. We are triumphant. We take back our lands.

Then spies from the west arrive. Paullinus knows. He is coming. Silly him. We keep fighting. We out-

---

[48] *Uerulāmion*, which would have a meaning like "[the tribe or settlement] of the broad hand"

number him by thousands. Let them come. We will fight them and defeat them and regain ourselves.

But that is not what happens. Though our numbers are vast this defile is to our disadvantage. Paullinus has us trapped. His javelin throwers let fly, like a swarm of straight lines against the grey of sky. And again. And again. Ceaselessly, it seems. They form their wedges and come at us, their cavalry behind. They have us boxed. They slaughter our animals, our horses, to block our passage back the way we came. They spear our hounds, to see us withered and grieving. The golden eagle rips and tears and is only stopped when his brother is battered on the stones.

They murder us. Firstly, the women who are positioned at the boundary, then all of us. The people are dying, and the ravens are a black cloud of ancestral grief in the gloaming afternoon. The river is clogged with pale bodies, sightless eyes, the confused faces of dead children. We are at least eighty thousand massacred this day. The Budekeh and her daughters stuff themselves with henbane. They will stay here. That is good. Your ancestors. Spirits to guard the future. For if they were to live they would be taken to Rome and executed in the oppressors' lands. That would be wrong. Many of our people get away. Many fall on their swords. Many are caught and trapped and herded onto 'reservations'.

Paullinus sends word to Rome: *The whole army was then brought together and kept under canvas to finish the remainder of the war. The emperor strengthened the forces by sending from Germany two thousand legionaries, eight cohorts of auxiliaries, and a thousand cavalry. On their arrival the men of the ninth had their number made up with legionary soldiers. The allied infantry and cavalry were placed in new winter quarters, and whatever tribes still wavered or were hostile were ravaged with fire and sword.*[49]

---

[49] Tacitus, Annals, Book 14: 38

CHAPTER ELEVEN
Survival

70CE

Not thirty years beyond the end of the self-sovereignty of the indigenous priteneh Kelts the Roman-governor is Tacitus' father-in-law Gnaeus Julius Agricola. I would say that by now, he and Tacitus are thick as thieves, and our stories tarnished to suit the politics.

While governor of what is now proclaimed Britannia, Agricola entertains a shadowy figure, a banished Irish exiled clansman, Feradach Fechtnach[50], who requests that Agricola helps him regain his lands and riches. Although Rome never conquers Ireland, or even

---

[50] The British Chronicles, Volume 1, David Hughes, 2007

makes a perceivable mark there, doesn't mean another traitor didn't open the door. Just so you know. What the Romans did to us, the future hybrid of cultures, called the English will perpetuate onto Ireland, and from there to other cultures around the world.

Kartimandweh, now Roman client regent of the Brijantax you will remember, and traitor to Caradoc, just gets worse. She has a husband named Uenusheh[51] whom she divorces. He takes up arms against her, for she is thoroughly Romanized, and he cannot stand it anymore. Rome sends troops to defend their client queen. When insurrection continues she is eventually evacuated. Uenusheh has taken back our lands. We live within the fortified ditches and ramparts of what will be one day known as Stanwick Camp, in what will be called North Yorkshire. We celebrate the victory against Rome. We re-mantle Uenusheh as *wosaljaxto*.

---

[51] Venutius. Later a guerilla fighter against Roman occupation, possibly of the Carveteh tribe, now Cumbria

We, Brijanteh lands and ancestors, want our freedom back. Rome, predictably, will not give it.

Now, in 71CE Quintus Petillius Cerialis arrives to take command. Another one. My stars, they go through emperors like diarrhea. He decides us upstart Brijantach need to come to heel, like their hounds that they must threaten and cower and not honor as we do with our relatives. He wars with us. He does not realize that we will fight him for decades.

ORDOVIKEH NOT OUT... THEN OUT

Before Agricola comes we, the Ordovikeh, destroy the cavalry and encampments that have sprung up like maggots on a corpse. The word is disseminated to the other tribes and hope is a silence spread across the land where every living thing and sacred stone holds a breath, and watches, and asks *What will be? Do we dare?*

Agricola summons veterans and more and more and

more. We stay in the mountains. *This is us, we say. You go!* We roar. But they don't.

Agricola brings his savagery and his butchery to us. Blood upon the sacred stones, us becoming grass and river and the new bud of the rowan and the apple after the blossoms of the spring of every year. Don't they understand we cannot die?

Inish Môn is as she was before Paullinus and so, again, like the seal and salmon, are once again a threat because we wear human form. Agricola comes just as Paullinus once did. Again, we die in the shapes of women and men, child and elder, druid and wizard and shaman. Again, the susurration of the waves licks the stones clean of our bodies and we become Manannán mac Lír.

CHAPTER TWELVE
Monarch of the Glen

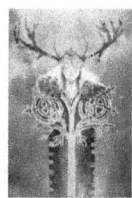

ALBA (SCOTLAND) NOT OUT

And there I am, silver, still, within my winter fur, lapping at the lake when, from across the predawn whiteness comes the scream of vixen, *bansídhe*[52] demanding we mate. My tail becomes my talisman now. I must admit I moan because this could take all day and I'll be bitten time and time again. But puppies!

And Badger in our burrows smell the melt and venture forth with our children. Swallow, like laughter, dart too fast for even me to bother with, can

---

[52] feminized (ban) genus loci (sídhe), it has been said...

keep their flight while I hunt Stoat and Martin from my perch upon this crag that formed before the forests here, of oak and ash and rowan and thorn; that formed with the glaciers and has carried my chicks to Eagle ever since.

Below and all about we rustle and caw and slide gently over yarrow leaving silver trails, and gather pollen from amidst the new young gorse and hop from stone to stone amongst the rumble of rocks within the gurgle of the burn.

Close by, within the druid forests, an army of us gather, sniffing at each other, braiding each other's hair, fucking when we get a moment, eating from Boar on the spit, sharpening swords and polishing gold and silver torques. The bluest of the blue strut by the fires, laughing, our totems close, aware of their brothers and sisters, children, mothers and fathers, the scent of our breast milk, and furs a comforting damp.

The centurion is pulled from within the wicker cage

and dragged, terrified, his eyes as round as apples, towards the tannin waters of the bog. He is loaded with silver and gemstones. His person is adorned with the gifts of the people. He does not belong here. His smell is that of another land and an alien concept. Our women are the shadowy owls. It is they who kneel on the grass that fringes the bog. It is they who crush his skull and pull tight the cord that strangles him, that drive the sword between his ribs and send him into the deep dark where all life begins, whether womb or depth of night. We don't have a thing to say. She knows. We either live or die, it's all the same, but we give a gift before us to mark the occasion.

KALAKASH (CALGACUS)
CHIEFTAIN OF THE KALEDON – 84CE

It has been suggested, by several scholars, that Tacitus made up the following speech. He, now in his thirties, is still with his father-in law (Agricola), now becoming an old man and desiring another battle or slaughter or conquest—whatever—because one of his children has just died, and he needs to vent. The

Romans consider grief a "woman's thing", instead preferring violence. But why would Tacitus invent this? He is right here. Our Biketeh (P/Bictish) chieftain is right here. We are the sole unconquered Keltic priteni tribe. And we are not about to allow this upstart, or his troops that glitter and preen, to change this. So, read for yourselves and decide:

"THEY MAKE A WASTELAND AND CALL IT PEACE"

Whenever I consider the origin of this war and the necessities of our position, I have a sure confidence that this day, and this union of yours, will be the beginning of freedom to the whole of Britain. To all of us slavery is a thing unknown; there are no lands beyond us, and even the sea is not safe, menaced as we are by a Roman fleet. And thus in war and battle, in which the brave find glory, even the coward will find safety. Former contests, in which, with varying fortune, the Romans were resisted, still left in us a last hope of succor, inasmuch as being the most renowned nation of Britain, dwelling in the very heart of the country, and out of sight of the shores of the conquered, we could keep even our eyes unpolluted by the contagion of slavery. To us who dwell on the uttermost confines of the earth and of freedom, this remote sanctuary of Britain's glory has up to this time been a defence. Now, however, the furthest limits of Britain are thrown open, and the unknown always passes for the marvellous. But there are no tribes beyond us, nothing indeed but waves and rocks, and the yet more terrible Romans, from whose oppression escape is vainly sought by obedience and submission. Robbers of the world, having by their universal plunder exhausted the land, they rifle the deep. If the enemy be rich, they are rapacious; if he be poor, they lust for dominion; neither the east nor the west has been able to satisfy them. Alone among men they covet with equal eagerness poverty and riches. To robbery, slaughter, plunder, they give the lying name of empire; they make a wasteland and call it peace (ubi solitudinem faciunt, pacem appellant).

Nature has willed that every person's children and

kindred should be their dearest objects. Yet these are torn from us by conscriptions to be slaves elsewhere. Our wives and our sisters, even though they may escape violation from the enemy, are dishonoured under the names of friendship and hospitality. Our goods and fortunes they collect for their tribute, our harvests for their granaries. Our very hands and bodies, under the lash and in the midst of insult, are worn down by the toil of clearing forests and morasses. Creatures born to slavery are sold once and for all, and are, moreover, fed by their masters; but Britain is daily purchasing, is daily feeding, her own enslaved people. And as in a household the last comer among the slaves is always the butt of his companions, so we in a world long used to slavery, as the newest and most contemptible, are marked out for destruction. We have neither fruitful plains, nor mines, nor harbours, for the working of which we may be spared. Valour, too, and high spirit in subjects, are offensive to rulers; besides, remoteness and seclusion, while they give safety, provoke suspicion. Since then you cannot hope for quarter, take courage, I beseech you, whether it be safety or renown that you hold most precious. Under a woman's leadership the Brigantes were able to burn a colony, to storm a camp, and had not success ended in supineness, might have thrown off the yoke. Let us, then, a fresh and unconquered people, never likely to abuse our freedom, show forthwith at the very first onset what heroes Caledonia has in reserve.

Do you suppose that the Romans will be as brave in war as they are licentious in peace? To our strifes and discords they owe their fame, and they turn the errors of an enemy to the renown of their own army, an army which, composed as it is of every variety of nations, is held together by success and will be broken up by disaster. These Gauls and Germans, and, I blush to say, these Britons, who, though they lend their lives to support a stranger's rule, have been its enemies longer than its subjects, you cannot imagine to be bound by fidelity and affection. Fear and terror there certainly are, feeble bonds of attachment; remove them, and those who have ceased to fear will begin to hate. All the incentives to victory are on our side. The Romans have no wives to kindle their courage; no parents to taunt them with flight, man have either no country or one far away. Few in number, dismayed by their ignorance, looking around upon a sky, a sea, and forests which are all unfamiliar to them; hemmed in, as it were, and enmeshed, the Gods have delivered them into our hands. Be not frightened by the idle display, by the glitter of gold and of silver, which can neither protect nor wound. In the very ranks of the enemy we shall find our own forces. Britons will acknowledge their own cause; Gauls will remember past freedom; the other Germans will abandon them, as but lately did the Usipii. Behind them there is nothing to dread. The forts are ungarrisoned; the colonies in the hands of aged men; what with disloyal subjects and oppressive rulers, the towns are ill-affected and rife with discord. On the one side you have a general and an army; on the other, tribute, the mines, and all the other penalties of an enslaved people. Whether you endure these forever, or instantly avenge them, this field is to decide. Think, therefore, as you advance to battle, at once of your ancestors and of your posterity. [53]

They have been raiding our grain supplies. Unclean thing to do. It's alright when it is us, the people, taking from the people, because we will raid their cattle anyway, but no. This stranger has no right. We send messengers telling them to fuck off. They are taken prisoner, or they are skinned alive. What kind of rules are these? Then they are here.

We are thirty thousand strong. We summon the spirits of our ancestors, the land, the wild boar, eagles riding thermals overhead, the seven-tined stag watching from that crest. We summon the strength of mother bear and the speed of the lynx. Our druids dance and sing into the night, wandering the twilight worlds where stories dwell, and ghosts feed us with their

---

[53] This translation is from the Latin. Tacitus *Agricola*, Book 1, 30 to 33. It is obviously an adaptation or invention, due to the use of Romanised wording

misty breath. The crags and burns, thistle and fords say keep us safe. Our home. Rome has no right within these mountains and these valleys, for we are here since forever, no matter what history will say. There is no *terra nullius*[54]. We have not come from somewhere else. We are this earth. These standing stones. We are bred from heather and broom.

We fight them for weeks. It is exhausting. They assume wrong. They think to starve us out by emptying our granaries, wherein all they do with that is cause annoyance. Our bannock is not our main fare. Our brothers and sisters of flesh, in exchange for that of our own when the time comes to die, that's the way of life and death. We drink the *uisge beatha*[55] and it keeps the cold away; makes us happy and horny.

The last day of fighting is at a place that Rome will

---

[54] Country not inhabited, Used to excuse colonization worldwide.

[55] Whisky, literally *water of life*

call Mons Graupius, but that we don't. It is simply home.

Although we sent three hundred and sixty of their soldiers to the earth and river depths, our dead and injured number ten thousand. So be it. We have retreated deeper into the landscape. We can no longer be seen. Deeply within our territories, amidst the holly and the fir, and the sweet water bubbling from the womb of mother earth, we take up our lives again. For no one and nothing, not bred or bouldered within these heartlands, can survive it, let alone thrive.

POSTSCRIPT

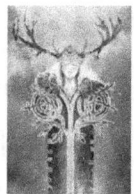

Forty years later Rome still cannot overcome us, and so the emperor Hadrian builds a wall to, symbolically, keep us out of the subjugated lands.

Rome says all the lands of the Keltic people are theirs—conquered—the same, they boast, of the people. But we cannot, in truth, be owned. It is a concept we do not comprehend. They build settlements and cities. Develop what does not need development. Take our homes. Build roads, buildings, temples, more buildings and more buildings. They cut down the forests and… well I don't know where I am.

Rome trades with Germanic people, with everyone,

really, because they enslave most of it. How can such a little place do that? The Saxons invade three hundred years after our firebrand is quelled and we no longer know how to defend our territory. Beaten, bred out, and traded as cattle. How can we lift our heads? Do the storytellers secretly keep our lore? Are they out there somewhere? Are we free anywhere? Of course, we are.

Saxons invade with the intention of colonisation. Rome manages to drive that initial invasion and land grab from our shores, but the Roman *imperium* is now the mere shadow of the bully it once was, and it withdraws the military from our lands, four hundred years beyond our ultimate historic invisibility.

We are still hunters. Our horses know us. Our hounds. We and the boar still eat each other. Brother bear, sister wolf, mother owl and father otter, salmon cousins and mackerel, seabirds and their eggs know our feet upon the cliff side. But iron does not know us in the shape of the sword except in the north and in secrecy elsewhere. Openly train our sons and daughters? No. Our daughters no longer wear the boar tusk or the kill feather. Deeply wrong.

Four hundred years after Budekeh, come new and ceaseless waves of invasion and alien settlement. Jutes[56] come. We don't fight. We don't know what to do. The Angles[57] come: first mercenaries and then, when Rome departs for good, the invaders settle and breed. They stay. They are more than us. In 450CE more and more of the same keep coming. They settle in vast numbers in and around Kent. They claim it as a kingdom, not a Kenteh anymore. They spread out.

In 597CE a *catholic* pope, a man named Gregory, decides that the remaining Britons, no longer tattooed, but still very decidedly *heathen*—is to be

---

[56] Jutland is Denmark/Germany

[57] South Denmark. Angle is where the word England derives.

drawn into the cult of the dead god. He sends forty missionaries. Under the protection of the Saxon king Æthelberht to the east. Wallowing and enjoying the luxuries left by Rome, they somehow manage to convince people that their religion is real. How? Æthelberht has cut a deal.

They are driven out, sensibly, by the sons of Æthelberht and another king, Sæberht of Essex, at the time of their fathers' deaths, reintroducing their many deities. But one king, Rædwald of East Anglia, retains his belief. Eventually, by the first half of the seventh century, they are back. And that is that. Spread like lice. Stupidity gained by way of a hostile sword.

You and I are not included. We have reclaimed the ink, are still the 'painted people'. But not for another thousand years. We are no longer part of this story.

Anglo-Saxon rule is imposed. The Keltic Britons are

driven to the margins of our lands or bred out, or force-married, or simply absorbed, the colour faded from us, sometimes even love. For are we not the people who have known these other people for thousands of years? We were never meant to be enemies. The Seven Kingdoms form: East Anglia, Essex, Kent, Mercia, Northumbria and Wessex.

There. We are obliterated from the history books.

The Vikings come in 793CE.

England is exponentially Christian.

The Normans come in 1066, during the *crusades*, an excuse to re-occupy Palestine and Jerusalem. Essentially also a land-grab by both the church of Rome and their Norman allies, of those sanction as 'in charge' who leave their *tuaths* and land holdings to those not equipped to defend them.

Kelts no longer shine within the light of brother sun and mother moon. The Anglo-Saxons (the English) do. When the English are dying on the road to Jerusalem the French, at the hand of greedy church officials, are given their lands and their estates. England becomes France, becomes England. Becomes an alien thing. And here is where I stop. This is almost the whole of the story. It seems so grim, does it not?

But I have much to lift your spirit... Remember what Keltic scholar Anne Ross said? *"...the Kelts were so completely engrossed with, and preoccupied by, their religion and its expression that it was constantly and positively[58] at the forefront of their lives."*

As an animal species we are self-aware, and we can self-reflect. That is not in difference to other species of animal, plant, stone or sky.

But you and I *know* we are animals. That we are the same animal that subjects its own kind to intentional violence and unspeakable cruelty is unbelievable to both you and me. That the species known as 'man'

---
[58] Italics mine

perpetrates that cruelty, whether calculatedly or unconsciously on other species, whether brother horse and tree or sister stone, sister hen, mother river, father otter or grandmother air is beyond our comprehension. I sit here looking out this window at the winter day. Filigreed trees and a sky pearlescent with hues of silver and light blue. Just days since midwinter solstice, the moon a pale crescent to the east, even this early in the afternoon. We are beauty within a city, ten thousand miles from the lands of our ancestors.

What happened to us within those lands is a tragedy of poverty and desolation? Just like Wounded Knee and the Black Hills, just like Slaughterhouse Creek.

There is no 'spirit world', just a world, and wondrous and mysterious she is, this ancestor-mother. I do not concede a separation. I recognize differences and they delight. I am aware that in 2015CE, at an event on Tasmania Island, called DARK MOFO[59] forty-three

---

[59] MONA, Hobart. Midwinter festival.

thousand people attend the midwinter feast and fifteen hundred people take to the river at dawn in a ritual as old as the time, when we were p/briteneh still. This is the day of the Kelt.

We are still here and, while we may recoil in anguish at a world of suffering, where refugees from Syria, Sudan, Iraq and Myanmar wander the earth in search of home, a right to live without brutality, where Pacific islands sink, and arctic ice recedes, in an age of volcanoes and earthquakes and in an eon when the white fox and the black bear no longer communicate with us or we with them, no longer roam at will through forests under snow, we are listening, mother. Mother, we remember. Suffering *hireath*[60].

We are still here, and our roots are deep. Many of us have been sent or relocated, to Australia, to America, to Canada, to the Caribbean, to New Zealand… as far from our *tuaths* and dolmen and standing stones as is conceivable. But this is one earth and one sky, and the

---

[60] Welsh for a homesickness or longing that cannot be assuaged.

oceans carry messages as do the rain and wind. So it doesn't matter. What matters is this knowledge because without it we are nothing. As with every other indigenous people everywhere our music, language, culture, kinship systems, law and lore have been violated, misrepresented, undervalued and made illegal. When we met or are yet to meet), and you *quicken* and we understand that these stories are what unite us (within the magic) it means that, should they need to know, our children and their children into the mists will have this. We know there are many others, many books, and many articles. But they always say, "the Kelts were..."

AUTHOR'S NOTE
INK

I was first tattooed thirty years ago. A crescent moon. I am now heavily tattooed. It seemed a radical step to ink my forehead with the symbols I consider relevant, but I went ahead with it anyway. Both my hands are inked with designs, Keltic work. The man who inked my forehead is now dead. At first, he was afraid. That was peculiar. Why, I asked. Because it's illegal, he said. What? Yes, Ly, some obscure British law. What is it? Um... it states that it's illegal to tattoo the hands and the face 'because,' he said, 'it's illegal to deface the property of the *crown*.'

THE TRIBES OF B/PRITENI PEOPLE

The places and names are Romanized. Please adjust)

THE SOUTH LANDS

Catuvellauni – Just inland from the east coast, Hertforshire, Bedfordshire, Cambridgeshire.

Trinovantes – East central coast, bordering the Ekeneh

E/Iceni – East central coast Britain

Atrebates – South central Britain – Hampshire, Sussex, Berkshire

Belgae – Southern Britain, Northern France. Also equated to the Irish Firbolg by O'Rahilly[61]

Cantiaci – East coast, Kent

Durotriges – Southern Britain, Dorset and Wiltshire

Dumnonii – Southwest Britain – Devon and Cornwall

Dobunni – Southwest Britain, North Somerset to

---

[61] See bibliography

Oxfordshire.

THE HEART

Brigantes – The whole of Northwest Kelts (and I have a sister tribe in Ireland). The other power in the heartlands are the Coritani (Corieltauvi) who dwell in most of the east Midlands from Lincolnshire to Northamptonshire, including Nottinghamshire.

The other tribes, mentioned below, would have been part of the confederacy.

Cornovii – Midwest, bridging the border of what is now England and Wales

Parisii – East Riding, Yorkshire, far northeast coast

THE NORTH

Caledonii – Most of Albion. The tribes mentioned below are only mentioned by Ptolemy and are most like small confederacies of the Caledonii. The Caledonii would have been the people known as Picts and their most common kindred, the Irish.

Caereni – Sutherland, west coast of Albion

Carnonacae – Rothshire, west coast of Albion

Cornovii – Caithness, northern Albion

Creones – Isle of Skye

Decantae – Cromarty Firth, western Albion

Epidii – (Epidion) Far west coast of Albion and associated with the isle of Islay

Smertae – North central Albion (see the burial cairn of Càrn Smeart)

Taexali – North eastern coast of Albion

Vacomagi – Strathsprey, on the coast of Albion

Venicones – Six miles east of Dundee, Albion

Votadini – Southeast Albion

THE WEST (NOT INCLUDING IRELAND) – WALES

Ordovices – Central west Wales. This tribe and the Silures (southeast Wales) were the main tribes of the west. The two tribes mentioned below Silures are only mentioned by Ptolemy. They are most likely confederacies of the above.

Deceangli – Northern Wales

Demetae – Southwest Wales

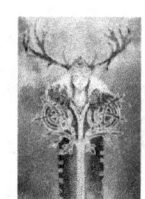

BIBLIOGRAPHY

Caesar, Julius, *Bellum Gallicum, 58-49BCE*

Campbell, J. *Masks of God: Occidental Mythology*, Penguin Books, NY, USA, 1982.

Condren, M. *The Serpent and the Goddess: Women, Religion and Power in Keltic Ireland*, New Island Books, 2002.

Cowan, T. *Fire in the Head, Shamanism and the Keltic Spirit*, HarperCollins, USA, 1993

Cowan, T. *Yearning for the Wind: Keltic Reflections on Nature and the Soul*, New World Library, 2003

Cunliffe, B. *The Keltic World*, Greenwich House, NY, 1986

Cruden, L. *Walking the Maze,* Destiny Books, USA, 1998

Eisler, R. *The Chalice and the Blade*, Harper, San Francisco, USA, 1988.

Eliade, M. *Shaman*, Bollingen Foundation, 1964

Foster, S. *Picts, Gaels and Scots*, Birlinn Limited, Scotland, 1996

Gantz, J. (translator, author anonymous), *Mabinogion*, Penguin Classics, USA, 1976

Gimbutas, M. *The Gods and Goddesses of Old Europe*, Thames and Hudson, UK, 1974.

Ginnell, L. *The Brehon Laws: A Legal Handbook*, www.forgottenbooks.org

James, S. *The World of the Kelts*, Thames and Hudson, 2005

Jordan, M. *Gods of the Earth*, Bantam Press, London, UK, 1992.

Malvern, M. *Venus in Sackcloth*, Southern Illinois Press, USA, 1975.

Markdale, J. *The Kelts,* Inner Traditions, USA, 1986

Markale, J. *Women of the Kelts,* Rochester, USA, 1986

Matthews, C. *The Keltic Tradition*, Shaftsbury, UK, 1989

O'Rahilly, T. F. *Early Irish History and Mythology*, Dublin Institute for Advanced Studies, 1964

Prior, F. *Britain BC*, HarperCollins Ebook only, 2011

Restall-Orr, E. *Living Druidry*, Piatkus Books, UK, 2004

Redgrove, P. *The Black Goddess and the Unseen Reality*, Grove Press, NY, USA, 1988.

Ross, A. Dr. *Druids, Preachers of Immortality*, The History Press, UK, 2013

Ross, A. Dr. *Pagan Keltic Britain*, Columbia University Press, 1967

Russel, M. *Bloodline,* Amberley Publishing, UK, 2010

Rutherford, W. *Keltic Lore*, HarperCollins, UK, 1993

Spence, L. *Magi Arts in Keltic Britain,* Rider, NY, 1945

Squire, C. *Keltic myths and Legends*, Random House, USA, 1994

Stone, M. *When God was a Woman*, Dial Press, NY, USA, 1976.

Tacitus, *Agricola*

Tacitus, *Annals*

APPENDIX 1

Please note, the term CE is used to describe what is known as the *Current Era* (in difference to AD, which is not appropriate) It is for conceptualizing an historic timeline, and of no consequence outside of that context.

ROMAN-GIVEN NAME	PRONUNCIATION (to the best research can attest)
Priteni	B/Priten-eh
Cantiaci	Kant-eh
Catuvellunii	Katuvallunneh
Kloutābona	Klotayboon-eh
Durotrigues	Durratrijah
Caledonii	Kaledonax
Cassivellaunus	Kashevel-lunnish
Segovii	Shejoveh
Comius	Komyush
Nemetocenna	Nemetahkeneh
Atrebates	Atrebatesh
Trinovantes	Trinovanteh

Imanuentius	Imanuentiwesh
Ekeneh/Iceni	Ekeneh
Cunobelinus	Kymbelineh
Caradoc	Karadoch
Brigantian	B/Pridjanshe
Briganti	B/Prijanteh
Camulodinum	Kamuloddun
Mandubracius	Mandubrakesh
Tasciovanus	Taskyavanesh
Ordovices	Ordovikeh
Helios	Helyesh
Togodumnus	Tohadumnesh
Adminius	Adminish
Epaticcus	Eb/patekesh
Verica	Verikeh
Silures	Shiluresh
Dumnonii	Dumnonach/eh
Caledonii	Kaledoneh/ax
Prasutagus	Brashetahesh
Cartimandua	Kartimandweh
Calgacus	Kalakash
Deceanglii	Dekanjleh

NOTE

(see Appendix 2 for more)

-ach on the end of a people/place name = *as*. This represents a non-separation from the lived environment. A process only understood, in the current era, by indigenous people who have a continuous ancestry with place.

-ax = is a plural, indicating a group, for example the Shejovax (Segovici)

-eh = is similar to é, insofar as elongates the final consonant only. The Romans have added -i or -ii (plural), therefore Ekeneh (Ekeneh) is actually Ekenn)

-ash, -esh and -ish on the end of a word is as -ach.

Keltic dialect does not use an -es sound. Pronunciation is -sh. They also do not pronounce -th or -p, the latter being a soft -b.

-ch is not guttural, but is spoken as with the word *loch*.

There is no hard -g sound. -g is as -j, as in bridge or, as for Toghodumnus and Imbolg, an -h sound, or even simply -e.. So Tohodumnesh and Imelech.

-u is always pronounced -oo, so that a dun (fortress) is *doon*, but soft, almost non-existent, as in Edinborough (edn-borough) or Dunedin (dn-eden) (same word)

Most Keltic words pronounce the emphases on the first consonant, so Moran (as a name) is mOren, not morAn. (and by the way Mor is Irish for *big*).

The loss of pronunciation is the loss of tongue. It affects the synapses and agrees to the usurpation and conquerage of indigenous voices.

Keltic people are non-literate, not illiterate. Please be aware, when researching, that most documents are written by people who are thoroughly christianised, and that many early, medieval documents are written by monks.

APPENDIX 2

From *Witch | For Those Who Are*, 2018

So, to *bandraíodóir* (Sometimes said to mean originally 'coming from or belonging to the sea,' because that was supposed to be the stopping place of the soul before birth or after death [Barnhart]; if so, it would be from Proto-Germanic *saiwaz. Klein explains this as "from the lake," as a dwelling-place of souls in ancient northern Europe)

Caillea-ch (as a word because it is not a name, and *as the circle, mistranslated as old hag, or ugly old woman*) is interesting, but not in the way most every site online, and most books describes it. *calleach* is purported to be an anthropomorphic feminized spirit of place, incorrectly termed a *deity*, with the meaning of an anthropomorphic and separately binary gendered, out-there, non-landscape, weather, seasonal person-seeming something. As an old hag. There is a wild promontory on the cliffs of Moher, Ireland, named Ceann Caillí interpreted as Hag's Head, also, in Scotland *Cailleach Bheur(ach)* and is associated with winter. Argyle's *Cruachan* (Cruachan Mountain) is said to be the home of *cailleach nan cruachan*. Thinking as an animist, however, we can remove the androcentric association and realize that Ben Cruachan *is cailleach nan cruachan*. Can you see what I see that? All the places named for *cailleach* are *high*.

When ascertaining the potential threat of invasion or attack where do people want to be? High. Where they can see in a 360° circle. Also, in the cycle of a year winter always comes. There's been *so* much lost in translation.

The many ridiculous tales, from that patrician old man in the sky, from his poor tortured son and that son's virginal mother ascending, literally on a cloud, to that poor tortured son's lover living out the remainder of her life in a cave in Baum, France, drinking only her own tears for sixty years until she, too, ascends. There is no animism and as such real stories of weather gods, seasonal gods, gods of place have been belittled and dishonored. And the animists, the people of this knowledge, humiliated and called barbarians, and history writ by those believing themselves far superior when that's transparent ignorance.

In the *hag* testaments the *old woman* bit comes in because *hag* has an etymology: Early 13C: *repulsive old woman* (rare before 16C.) probably from Old English hægtes, hægtesse *witch, sorceress, enchantress, fury*. Dutch *heks,* German *Hexe witch.* The disambiguation is due, mistakenly, to a later Anglo-Saxon interpretation that, by then woman-shaming christianised monastics could not get their tonsures around. That of an animist language. To me the idea of winter as a person, with moods and mists and personality, is obvious.

English is a language of objectification. The language assumes there's us, and that everything else is *out there*. A language of nouns.

Dr. Robin Wall Kimmerer is a mother, scientist, writer, and Distinguished Teaching Professor of Environmental Biology at the SUNY College of Environmental Science and Forestry in Syracuse, New York. She is the founding Director of the Center for Native Peoples and the Environment; whose mission is to create programs that draw on the wisdom of both indigenous and scientific knowledge for our shared concerns for Mother Earth. She works at learning her language alongside her sister. She found it extremely difficult until she *grokked* it. She writes, in the essay *The Grammar of Animacy*: "To be a hill, to be a sandy beach, to be a Saturday, all are possible verbs in a world where everything is alive. Water, land, and even a day, the language a mirror for seeing the animacy of the world, the life that pulses through all things, through pines and nuthatches and mushrooms. *This* is the language we hear in the woods, this is the language that lets us speak of what wells up all around us. And the vestiges of boarding schools, soap-wielding missionary wraiths, hang their heads in defeat." [62]

Thus, realizing this, we return to Keltic/Gaelic and we learn that our word *calleach* is two words: The first part of the word *call, caill* or *cor*, means circle, as in *coracle,* a round boat. The end of the word, *ach* (pronounced as soft, like loch), is abstract but profound: the etymology (from Old Irish *-ach*, from Proto-Keltic *ākos*, compare Welsh -og. Doublet of -óg. Suffix –ach: *Forms nouns from other nouns and adjectives with the sense of 'person or thing connected or involved with, belonging to, having, as',* "Person or thing connected or involved with, belonging to, having, as." (Note: A *thing* is an ancient word for a gathering; an assembly of people for multiple purposes. It does not mean an object with no name).

---

[62] http://www.dailygood.org/more.php?n=6819

Éire (Ireland) + -ach→ Éireannach (*as* Ireland), Sasana (England)+ -ach→ Sasanach (*as* England) = sasanach, Albanach[i], for example is a person (no matter the species) from Alba = Albanach. We are the landscape. An ancient way of knowing still extant within indigenous people's language:

"To be a hill, to be a sandy beach, to be a Saturday, all are possible verbs in a world where everything is alive."

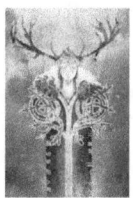

ACKNOWLEDGEMENTS

Thank you to Bernard J Casimir, genealogist, *The Signs of the Times*[63], for the light shone onto this strong thread of our ancestral history.

Instrumental to this work have been my long-lived friendships with: Nila Chandra and Eldritch Forest.

THIS BOOK IS FOR

My three children, their children, and those yet to be born.

---

[63] www.thesignsofthetimes.com.au

ABOUT THE AUTHOR

Ly de Angeles, writer, teacher, storyteller, psychic, has been in print since 1987 and is an award-winning author and filmmaker, director and producer of stage and screen, mother, grandmother, scholar, deep ecologist, mythographer, feminist, psychic and indigenous Kashuvellunneh woman. Her ancestor is Caradoc ap Kymbelineh.

Photograph Serenity de Angeles, Melbourne.

www.ingramcontent.com/pod-product-compliance
Lightning Source LLC
Chambersburg PA
CBHW052307300426
44110CB00035B/2165